BUILDING A CAREER IN SOFTWARE

A COMPREHENSIVE GUIDE TO SUCCESS IN THE SOFTWARE INDUSTRY

Daniel Heller

Apress®

Building a Career in Software: A Comprehensive Guide to Success in the Software Industry

Daniel Heller
Denver, CO, USA

ISBN-13 (pbk): 978-1-4842-6146-0   ISBN-13 (electronic): 978-1-4842-6147-7
https://doi.org/10.1007/978-1-4842-6147-7

Managing Director, Apress Media LLC: Welmoed Spahr
Acquisitions Editor: Shiva Ramachandran
Development Editor: Matthew Moodie
Coordinating Editor: Nancy Chen

Cover designed by eStudioCalamar

Distributed to the book trade worldwide by Springer Science+Business Media New York, 1 New York Plaza, New York, NY 100043. Phone 1-800-SPRINGER, fax (201) 348-4505, e-mail orders-ny@springer-sbm.com, or visit www.springeronline.com. Apress Media, LLC is a California LLC and the sole member (owner) is Springer Science + Business Media Finance Inc (SSBM Finance Inc). SSBM Finance Inc is a **Delaware** corporation.

For information on translations, please e-mail booktranslations@springernature.com; for reprint, paperback, or audio rights, please e-mail bookpermissions@springernature.com.

Apress titles may be purchased in bulk for academic, corporate, or promotional use. eBook versions and licenses are also available for most titles. For more information, reference our Print and eBook Bulk Sales web page at http://www.apress.com/bulk-sales.

Any source code or other supplementary material referenced by the author in this book is available to readers on GitHub via the book's product page, located at www.apress.com/9781484261460. For more detailed information, please visit http://www.apress.com/source-code.

Printed on acid-free paper

For my parents.

Contents

About the Author

Daniel Heller is a Staff Software Engineer in Infrastructure at a San Francisco based software company. In earlier lives, he has led reliability efforts on Uber Eats, built monitoring systems at AppDynamics, helped port iOS to the ARM64 architecture at Apple, directed the responses to dozens of high-stakes production outages, and managed teams of up to 25 engineers.

Along the way, the author discovered a love of mentorship and had the good fortune to mentor tens of talented engineers. Those engineers inspired him with their hundreds of questions about career paths, technical trade-offs, and day-to-day effectiveness; when a short blog post on those themes brought a riot of responses about maturing professionals' need for guidance, the author set out to fill the gap with this book.

Acknowledgments

I'm in the debt of Simon Newton, Angie Zhu, and Dave Pacheco for their encouragement to see this project through, their invaluable feedback on my first draft, and everything I've learned from witnessing their excellence.

Thanks as well to my intrepid early readers, Syrie Bianco, Andrew Mains, Carissa Blossom, Adam Cath, Marek Brysa, Dan Simmons, and Courtney Ryan; their feedback made a difference.

Thanks to Prashant Varanasi and Akshay Shah for an impactful nudge to get started at the beginning of the project.

By no means least, thanks to Matt Moodie and Shiva Ramachandran at Apress for their wonderful insight in shaping this mass of text into a book.

Introduction

In the last three years, I've realized that software engineers are starved for guidance about the professional world. I've spent those years working in a large team filled with bright, motivated programmers in the early years of their careers, and gradually, mentorship has come to be a huge part of my job. Most strikingly, engineers have taken me aside again and again and again to ask questions I recognize from the early, stressed-out days of my own career:

- Should I change jobs? Which job should I take?
- How do I grow as a technologist?
- What should I do when I don't agree with the technical decisions on my team?
- How can I make this meeting more effective?
- How should I prepare for my interview?
- How do I get promoted?
- How can I make this email better?
- How do I find a mentor?
- How do I mentor my junior colleague?
- What should I do when I'm on call and I don't know how to handle a problem?
- What areas should I focus on to be a better engineer?
- How do I deal with recruiters?
- …etc., etc., etc., etc., etc.

My colleagues' tremendous appetite for guidance has shown me that there's a critical gap in today's Computer Science education: young software engineers enter the industry with excellent technical preparation, but no one has taught them a darned thing about how to be a professional engineer—they have to teach themselves, and inevitably the hard way.

This book aims to fill that void with a professional manual for the aspiring software engineer, a guide to managers, role changes, professional technical practices, technical communication, meetings, on-call, project management, advancement, ongoing study, mentorship, compensation, and more.

For my part, I'm a software engineer at a major software company. I've been writing code and managing engineers for 12 years—I've worked at Apple, Uber, AppDynamics, and Microsoft (as an intern), managed teams of over 20 people, interviewed literally hundreds of engineers and managers, and been interviewed scores of times. I've written production JavaScript, Java, C++, Go, C, and assembly, shipped code in the web browser and the kernel, and led the responses to perhaps a hundred production outages. And I continue to do those things today; I'm not a consultant or an "architect" but a regular working coder, fixing bugs and debugging outages, trying to solve the toughest problems I can find with my code and my insight, because I enjoy it and think I do it reasonably well.

Most importantly for you, I'm not an especially gifted programmer; respectable definitely, above average on my good days, but I'm nothing like a 10x coder. So, I've made a fun and reasonably remunerative career on everything but coding brilliance—discipline, study, communication, project management, collaboration, prioritization, etc., etc., etc. This book will help you build your career the same way.

Part 1 is about careers: hiring, compensation, and promotion work in tech companies, how to best navigate those processes, and how to chart a course for growth and advancement.

Part 2 is about the sundry nontechnical skills that help you get traction in your daily work: project management, running meetings, working with your boss and peers, recovering from mistakes, team citizenship, and many other subjects I've found to challenge engineers in the workplace.

Part 3 goes deep on the single most important nontechnical skill for programmers: the sadly neglected art of engineering communication. It starts with a holistic model of communicating at work, then moves on to practical treatments of topics like technical writing, email, and asking effective questions.

Finally, Part 4 is technical; it covers a carefully curated selection of technical subjects that I've found particularly difficult for new software engineers—the kinds of issues that come up every day in software offices and never in software classrooms.

This book strives to offer you the best possible returns on your time; it treats a wide range of subjects with short, stand-alone sections friendly to random access as well as cover-to-cover reading. I hope it will arm you with the tools to steer your career with confidence, save you some or all of the mistakes that taught me my lessons, and ultimately help you succeed as a professional in software.

Career

The Big Picture

If You Only Take Away One Thing

Here's the most important lesson in this whole book: you need to own your own career, because no one else will guide you. Good mentorship can be wonderful for the .01% of engineers who find it, but in all likelihood, you are going to teach yourself 99% of everything you'll learn as a professional; great projects may fall into your lap once in a blue moon, but more often, you'll have to find your way to them yourself. Therefore, the most important tools in your toolbox are going to be personal responsibility and initiative; those qualities are what make you a trustworthy (and valued) professional, but also how you grow and advance. We'll discuss this principle in many contexts throughout the book.

What Is the Job?

Software engineers design, build, debug, and maintain software systems, which is to say they write text that tells computers to do useful things. At the time of this writing, these skills are some of the most sought-after in the global economy.

This work can take many forms. Some engineers are generalists, with the skills to make changes in almost any system, while some are specialists with profound expertise in one area; some maintain and improve existing systems, while some write new ones from scratch; some move from project to project, getting things working and moving on, while others own and develop one system for years. Some of us work at companies whose main product is

© Daniel Heller 2020

D. Heller, *Building a Career in Software*, https://doi.org/10.1007/978-1-4842-6147-7_1

software, while others work on ancillary systems to help produce a non-software product or service. Day to day, though, the foremost qualities of our work are more or less the same:

- We write a lot of code.

- Almost as much, and sometimes more, we debug code (analyze why things are going wrong).

- We work normal-ish hours (9–5 or 10–6), with extra hours tacked on at more intense companies and an hour lopped off here or there at slower shops.

- Collaboration is a big part of our jobs: we coordinate with other engineers, product managers, customers, operations teams, and etc., etc., etc.

- We write frequently for humans: design proposals, status updates, defect postmortems.

What It Means to Grow

Engineering is the enterprise of building and applying technology to solve problems, and I find joy and comfort in the observation that whatever the pros or cons of any one project, the world needs people who build things. My definition of growth derives from this observation: if we exist to solve problems, then growth is being able to solve more, tougher, and bigger problems. We do so with a vector of skills built over time:

- **Coding**: Clarity, testing, documentation, discipline in scope of diffs.

- **Project management**: Identifying dependencies, updating stakeholders, tracking tasks.

- **Communication**: Clear emails, engaging presentations, evangelizing our ideas.

- **Personal organization and time management**: Not dropping balls, prioritizing effectively.

- **Architecture**: The macroscopic design of systems.

- **Leadership/mentorship** at a level appropriate to their position.

- **Emotional skills**: Empathy, confidence, stress management, work–life balance.

Developing on each of those dimensions is certainly growth. And when we apply those skills successfully, we enjoy four pleasing and necessary benefits:

- Money
- Respect
- Title (bureaucratic blessings)
- Fulfillment, pride, and a sense of purpose

Acquiring each of the above is satisfying and practically beneficial. All of the preceding skills can be dissected in great detail, and much of this book does exactly that. I ask you to remember, though, that everything derives from our essential raison d'être as problem-solvers: the world needs problems solved, so companies need engineers who can solve them, so our impact is the foundation of our career progress.

Ten Principles

I once gave up a team to a new manager. Reflecting on our time together, and thinking about what I'd taught well and poorly as a manager, I wrote a short essay about the most critical practices that I think lift a newly minted software engineer from amateur to seasoned professional: the path from fixing bugs as an "Engineer 1" to leading major projects as a "Senior Engineer."

I was shocked by how strongly people responded to that little list of practices—it seems to be a hard-to-find lesson. It still captures what I see as the most important principles for personal growth and building a successful career, and I'll reproduce it here to set out the principles that thread through the more specific advice later in the book. These are the most important lessons that I wish I had learned years earlier than I did; I sure wish someone had sent it to me when I was 22.

1. **Reason about business value**: Reason like a CEO. Understand the value of your work to your company, and take responsibility for reasoning about quality, feature richness, and speed. Your job isn't just to write code; your job is to make good decisions and help your company succeed, and that requires understanding what really matters.

2. **Unblock yourself**: Learn to never, ever accept being blocked; find a way by persuasion, escalation, or technical creativity. Again, your job isn't just to write the code and wait for everything else to fall into place; your job is to figure out how to create value with your efforts.

3. **Take initiative**: The most common misconception in software is that there are grown-ups out there who are on top of things. Own your team's and company's mission. Don't wait to be told; think about what needs doing and do it or advocate for it. Managers depend on the creativity and intelligence of their engineers, not figuring it all out themselves.

4. **Improve your writing**: Crisp technical writing eases collaboration and greatly improves your ability to persuade, inform, and teach. Remember who your audience is and what they know, write clearly and concisely, and almost always include a tl;dr above the fold.

5. **Own your project management**: Understand the dependency graph for your project, ensure key pieces have owners, write good summaries of plans and status, and proactively inform stakeholders of plans and progress. Practice running meetings! All this enables you to take on much bigger projects and is great preparation for leadership.

6. **Own your education**: Pursue mastery of your craft. Your career should be a journey of constant growth, but no one else will ensure that you grow. Find a way to make learning part of your daily life (even 5 minutes/day); get on mailing lists, find papers and books that are worth reading, and read the manual cover to cover for technologies you work with. Consistency is key; build habits that will keep you growing throughout your career.

7. **Master your tools**: Mastery of editor, debugger, compiler, IDE, database, network tools, and Unix commands is incredibly empowering and likely the best way to increase your development speed. When you encounter a new technology or command, go deeper than you think you have to; you'll learn tricks that will serve you well again and again.

8. **Communicate proactively**: Regular, well-organized communication builds confidence and goodwill in collaborators; knowledge-sharing creates an atmosphere of learning and camaraderie. Share knowledge, and set a regular cadence of informing stakeholders on project goals, progress, and obstacles. Give talks and speak up judiciously in meetings.

9. **Find opportunities to collaborate**: Good collaboration both increases your leverage and improves your visibility in your organization. Advancing your craft as an engineer requires you to have an impact beyond the code you write, and advancing your career requires, to a certain degree, building a personal brand at your company. Cross-functional projects and professional, respectful collaboration are critical to both.

10. **Be professional and reliable**: Think of yourself as a professional, and act like one. Come to meetings on time and prepared, then pay attention. Deliver what you say you will, and communicate proactively when things go wrong (they will). Keep your cool, and express objections respectfully. Show your colleagues respect and appreciation. Minimize your complaining; bring the people around you up, not down. Everyone appreciates a true professional; more importantly, it's the right way to behave.

Your Relationship with Your Employer

Your company is your counterpart in a business transaction where you exchange your valuable skills for their valuable money—your employer is not your mother, your father, or your friend.

Like any firm doing business with another, your expectation should be that your company will make every decision out of rational self-interest. This profound truth has many important corollaries, foremost among them that

- Your company will never do anything for you out of sentiment.

- Your company doesn't owe you education, career development, a raise, or a long-term guarantee of employment.

- Everything your company does is business, not personal, and you shouldn't take it personally.

- You don't owe your company your personal loyalty—they certainly don't see themselves as owing you any.

- When you want something from your employer, you should approach it calmly, as a negotiation between two businesses.

None of these means you mistreat each other: like any two firms doing business, you aim to build a trust that allows for a long-running and mutually fruitful business relationship, and for both of you, building a good name as a trustworthy partner keeps other doors open.

We should approach our relationships with our employers calmly, without a sense of entitlement, aiming to follow our own ethics, firmly represent our interests, and secure the most favorable, mutually beneficial relationship we can. And if we can't get what we want, we shouldn't degrade ourselves by whining—we should sell our skills elsewhere on more favorable terms or accept our situations as the best available.

Landing Jobs

This chapter introduces hiring processes, interviews, and job offers—it aims to demystify the intimidating but mostly predictable journey from the wilderness to a job building software.

Many large tech companies' hiring systems are approximately the same. End to end, the process can take anywhere from < 1 week (for small startups where every stakeholder can get in a room on 5 minutes' notice) to multiple months (Google is famous in Silicon Valley for processes of 4–8 weeks with many stages of committee review). This section will outline the process, with subsequent sections treating each area in detail.

Before we begin, I'll note that smaller firms, especially early startups, often work very differently—they're much more likely to have informal, personality-driven processes, perhaps as simple as a conversation or meal with the team. Coding interviews are also anecdotally less prevalent outside of the United States.

The Recruitment Process

Resume Review and Recruiter Phone Screen

A recruiter screens your resume or LinkedIn profile. If they like what they see, they speak to you on the phone for 20–60 minutes, asking you questions about your interests, experience, and job/salary expectations. The recruiter then makes a decision about whether to pass a candidate on. They do not have technical expertise (though a hiring manager will have given them some

© Daniel Heller 2020

D. Heller, *Building a Career in Software*, https://doi.org/10.1007/978-1-4842-6147-7_2

keywords and context), so their decision is based on imperfect information, even relative to everyone else. Nevertheless, they have considerable discretion in whom to move forward with and whom to drop.

Technical Phone Screen(s)

You do one to two technical phone screens, each 45–60 minutes, with engineering managers and/or engineers. They ask you questions about your experience and likely have you write code in a shared editor like CodePair (or even a Google Doc).

On-site Interviews

You go to a company's office and do four to seven interviews of 45–60 minutes, each with one to three engineers or managers. You write code (either on a whiteboard or on a computer), design systems, and answer questions about your experience and interests. In between, you have lunch with a team.

Take-Home Coding Exercise

Not all companies use this stage. You're given a coding problem to work on for a few days on your own, then send the code to be reviewed by engineers.

Decision

Either a hiring manager or a committee makes the decision about whether to extend an offer. The committee may either be composed of interviewers and a hiring manager or drawn from a central committee (famously the custom at Google); generally, more senior/experienced committee members carry more weight.

The hiring meeting often begins with a simultaneous "thumbs up" or "thumbs down" from each committee member,[1] followed by a discussion to try to reach a consensus on whether to make a hire. The criteria are never objective in the sense of being measurable by a machine—instead, each committee member uses their intuition, sometimes against a written rubric of subjective criteria.

---

[1]Believed to reduce the risk that people will change their votes silently due to one strong voice; I don't think it does much.

Offer and Negotiation

A company's HR department and hiring manager (or in some cases, an independent committee) craft an offer. The main parameters of the offer are

- Level/title
- Base compensation
- Equity compensation
- Signing bonus and relocation
- Start date

All of these parameters are determined by your experience and interview performance (i.e., the company's perception of how valuable your work will be) and your competing offers, which they may try to match or beat.

Referrals

Companies usually have internal systems for employees to refer others for jobs; you may well be asked to refer others to your company or want to be referred elsewhere.

A referral with a strong personal endorsement is a big deal—it bumps a candidate to the head of the line at the screening stage, and if the referrer is well-regarded, it can make the difference at decision time. A corollary is that you should save your own strong referrals for people you trust—strong endorsements for bad hires reflect badly on you.

More casual referrals can nudge a resume into view in "Resume Review," but that's about it. I personally don't love making them myself (there isn't a lot of upside), but they aren't harmful if you're clear about your confidence level: "I know George from SprocketSoft; I didn't work with him extensively, but he's very interested in WidgetSoft."

Resumes

Resume formatting is not, in my experience, "make or break" of anything in tech—they can hurt a little, they can help a little, but the content speaks much more than the format. Still, there's no reason not to get them right. Below are the most important points; follow them, edit, tinker, and when you're done, get a peer review, ideally from a senior engineer or manager with interviewing experience. Let your friends, not a hiring manager, catch your mistakes.

Section Order

Sections should be ordered as experience, then skills, then education, because those are the priorities of hiring managers. That observation alone tells you something about the importance of internships for a student: they (usually) weigh more than coursework with hiring managers! If you're early in your career, you may elaborate more on your education (e.g., specific classes and projects); as you mature in the industry, you'll emphasize projects more and schooling less. Lots of people include hobbies; I think they're a nice-to-have and can safely be skipped.

Formatting

Resumes should be a single page. You can do it. If you are early in your career, you absolutely do not need more than one; the second page just says "I take myself too seriously" (hiring managers really will see it that way). Also, table gridlines give an appearance of amateurism (I can't exactly say why, but they do).

Tell a Story

Emphasize what you delivered, where you led, and the results your projects yielded: managers like signs of autonomy and leadership. Never say "Implemented features and bugfixes," which is well-known to be the most generic line ever added to an engineering resume; help the reader visualize you solving a big problem or taking a project from conception to delivery, not sitting passively at your desk waiting for someone to give you a bite-sized task.

Example

Below is an example of a junior engineer's resume; it's not a work of art, but if you're in doubt, you can copy this format.

JUNIOR S.E. NAME

youremailaddress@gmail.com (555) 555-5050 LinkedIn

Senior Computer Science student with experience in reliability engineering and web programming seeking challenging full-time position. Strong Java and Javascript programming skills and excellent communication.

EXPERIENCE

Acme Technologies *Software Engineering Intern*, Shopping Experience Team   06/2019–08/2019

- Built support for displaying per-product one-week trailing order counts in online store.
- Wrote Airflow workflow to compute order counts daily and load into production database.
- Extended gRPC product APIs to include order count.
- Built React component to display order count in store UI.

Verisimilar Software Systems *Software Engineering Intern*, Production Engineering Team 06/2018–08/2018

- Extending monitoring framework with support for microservices on experimental Kubernetes.
- Enhanced Python scripts for Grafana dashboard generation with Prometheus queries.
- Wrote Python templating framework for generating service alerts on Prometheus.

State Technical University Computer Science Department *Student Sysadmin*   10/2017–Present

- Administered lab of 50 Linux workstations for student use using Chef.
- Maintained NFS server for department use.
- Supported students and faculties with onboarding and account problems.

SKILLS

Programming Languages

Proficient: Java, Node.js/Javascript *Exposure:* Python, Go, C

Frameworks and Libraries

DropWizard, React/Redux, Apache Airflow, gRPC, TensorFlow

Infrastructure and Tools

Linux, Prometheus, Grafana, Kubernetes, Chef, IntelliJ, Chrome Dev Tools

EDUCATION

State Technical University

Bachelor of Science in Computer Science, GPA 3.84   Expected: 05/2020

Coursework:
Machine Learning, Operating Systems, Networking, Data Structures and Algorithms, Advanced Software Engineering, Computer Architecture, Discrete Mathematics

Projects:

- BookExchange: team of 3 built website in Node/React+MySQL for students to directly exchange textbooks.
- MoodClassifier: built deep neural network in TensorFlow to classify sentiment in movie reviews.
- MicroOS: worked in team of 2 to build Unix-like operating system in Java.

Extracurricular: Mentor for two freshman CS students, Vice President of Engineering Student Association

Home Town High School *Graduate, GPA 3.90*   09/2012–06/2016

Passing Engineering Interviews

This section is a brief overview of how to pass software engineering interviews. It will discuss what interviewers look for, what they'll ask, how to prepare, and how to behave during the interview. A later chapter will cover this subject from the interviewer's perspective. Whole books have been written on this subject, and as you look for your first job, you should read one (look at the Appendix to this section).

What They're Looking For

Software engineering interviews usually look for two things: ability and "culture fit." As we'll discuss in "Interviewing Software Engineers," neither is well understood, and neither is sought in a coherent way. However, you don't need to solve that problem for the industry: you need to pass interviews, which you can easily do with preparation.

Hiring managers look for several dimensions of ability. They are, in roughly decreasing order of priority

- Coding/debugging measured by coding on the fly in interviews and sometimes by a take-home coding problem

- Design/architecture measured by a design exercise in an interview

- Communication measured by how clearly you express your ideas in interviews

- Domain knowledge measured by factual questions and design exercises

"Culture fit," often and correctly maligned as a tool of conscious or subconscious discrimination, usually means three things:

- Enthusiasm for the role

- Positive attitude and friendliness

- Whatever interviewers happen to like

All three are measured by questions about your interests and goals and by the interviewers' general sense of your attitude.

The relative weights of domain knowledge, culture fit, and "raw ability" (i.e., coding and debugging) vary considerably by company and interviewer, but by and large, pure interview coding skill, that is, the ability to solve coding problems on the fly while talking about what you're doing in a pleasing way, is priority #1 for junior hires, and as of this writing, many companies are willing to give "smart people" a try at a specialization they haven't practiced before.

Acing Coding Interviews

For passing interviews, coding is king. That is to say, interview coding. Programming interviews are a kind of sanitized, stylized coding, a performance art where you have 30–60 minutes to solve a problem chosen by the interviewer while talking through your work; there's almost always some kind of tricky algorithmic problem at the core of the question.

You should on no account confuse interview coding with the day-to-day work of a software engineer, which is far messier, mostly driven by the behavior of existing code, mostly about integrations and debugging, and almost never about cracking a tricky algorithmic problem, which I personally do just a couple of times per year.

On my bad days, I'm outraged by the lack of realism of coding problems and the way they favor people who are blessed with the ability to be calm under pressure and a gift for oratory, neither being skills that come up on a daily basis when doing the real job. However, interviewers need to ask something, and while these interviews may not be that realistic, they are reasonably easy to prepare for; you should think of a coding interview as a performance art that you can easily excel at with practice.

Preparation

Here's how you prepare for technical interviews, in decreasing priority order; because coding interviews are fairly predictable, most engineers I know, no matter how experienced, prepare roughly the same way:

- Solve a bunch of coding problems, with real code, to get your brain in the groove of time-pressured problem-solving. Sites like leetcode.com have large banks of practice questions; question quality varies, but if you do 50 problems end to end, you'll be more than ready.

- Study your CS fundamentals, especially linked lists, hash tables, trees, sorting, and the (Big-O) analysis of the memory and runtime of all of the above. Brush up on dynamic programming if you're feeling energetic.

- Brush up on the specific domain of the job you're applying for, and prepare to discuss the standard technologies architectures in that space.

- Practice talking through what you're doing to get used to the performance aspect of interviewing; have a friend grill you in a mock interview if you can.

On the Day

Your primary goal in the coding interview is to solve the problem. As I've mentioned earlier, however, it's also a dramatic performance: interviewers want you to show them that you bring orderly reasoning to a technical problem and that you can communicate that reasoning to a collaborator. Luckily, what they're looking for is again pretty predictable.

- **Explain what you're doing**: Talk out loud. Explain what line of solution you're considering, what problems you think it might have, what the problem resembles from your past experience, what the tradeoffs are in your solution, etc. You want to take the interviewer on a journey with you, where they feel that they really understand and relate to your thought process all along the way. Even if you don't ace the problem, the interviewer should be able to say, "they expressed themselves really clearly. Even though they didn't quite finish, what they were trying made sense to me."

- **Start with a simple solution**: Unless you see the perfect solution instantly, it pays to start simple and iterate. Explain what you're starting with and why. It's much better to produce a solution that works inefficiently than to never solve the problem at all; professional engineers also take this approach in designing real systems.

- **Restate the problem and ask clarifying questions**: Interviewers love to see you refine the problem's requirements, because they show that you want to fully understand a problem before starting to code. Restating the problem is similar, and if you don't understand the problem correctly, the interviewer may set you on the right path.

- **Stay calm and never give up**: It's not a requirement that you nail, or even finish, every (or any) problem to get a job. Staying calm, trying a variety of approaches, talking through a sensible thought process, and recording whatever you manage to come up with can easily make up for an imperfect solution. Many interviewers ask questions that are almost impossible to completely finish and for which partial credit can be fine.

- **Code in a language you know well, and make that language Python if possible**: Otherwise Java. I program in Go in my day-to-day life, but I interview in Python; it's simply the best coding interview language, full stop. Here's the hierarchy from my experience:

  1. Python coders pass interviews; Python helps them with its dynamism, convenient collections, easy-to-use string helpers, and, above all, its conciseness.

  2. Java programmers get bogged down in the verbosity of defining a POJO[2] or the awkwardness of JSON parsing but probably get there in the end.

  3. Go programmers do pretty much the same as Java programmers.

  4. Scala, Clojure, and Haskell programmers write beautiful functional code but never quite get the problem working all the way, struggling with some obscure point of syntax, getting stuck on a simple bug their interviewer could help with if they knew the language, or slowed down too much by just-not-quite-right editing support.

  5. C and C++ programmers tend to run out of time getting a hash table to work right or some thing else that works effortlessly in Python.

  6. Perl programmers should understand the signal interviewing in Perl sends and seem to struggle with defining clean data types.

Passing the Rest of the Interview

If you've aced your technical interviews, you're most of the way to getting the job. In the rest of your conversations, you want to convey that you're excited about the job and company, that you're passionate about technology, and that you're a fun and pleasant person to work with. I suggest a few key tools:

- Prepare a compelling and specific answer to the question, "why do you want to work here?"—the answer should have something to say about both the company's business and its technology; for example, "I grew up with dogs, I have dogs now, and I actually use puppersoftware.com myself. I've also read several of the company's blog posts

---

[2]Plain Old Java Object

and was impressed with the JavaScript performance work you've done." You should spend at least an hour researching the company, especially reading their public technical writing and talks so you're ready to give credible answers.

- Try to balance humility (that you've enjoyed learning from people, that you know you make mistakes) with confidence (that you believe you can tackle big problems and are excited to do it).

- Show your enthusiasm for technology when you get the chance; mention a tool you love to use, a book that influenced you, etc.

- Don't badmouth your previous employer or colleagues, which shows only that you're sour and will badmouth this employer in the future.

- Prepare one or two questions about the company and team; at the end of every interview, interviewers will likely give you a chance to ask your own questions. A question highly specific to the team/company is ideal, but generic questions are fine too. A few good examples are

  - What do you think are the biggest technical problems you need to solve in the next year?

  - What's your favorite thing about working here?

  - What do you think your team does especially well, and where do you think you need to improve?

  - What do you think are the toughest problems facing your organization?

You should also do your best to be charming, that is, to create a positive feeling in your interviewers and put them at ease; I suggest at least smiling, shaking hands firmly, and expressing (truthful) enthusiasm whenever you can.

Further Reading

- Leetcode is an extremely convenient place to practice coding questions. The interface is useful, and the questions are realistic for interviews (though some are too hard and some are too easy). If I were going to interview for a job next week, the first thing I would do would be crank through a bunch of Leetcode problems.

- *Cracking the Coding Interview* is a well-known book of example programming interview questions. It's a good place to find examples.

Recruiters

This section will discuss who recruiters are and what you need to know about working with them, both as colleagues and on opposite sides of the table.

Recruiters are employees or contractors who help companies find and hire employees. This role exists for many fields, including medicine, law, and consulting; I'll speak only to tech recruiting, which has become quite polished in the tech boom[3] of the 2010s. Tech recruiters usually fall into three specializations, ordered here by increasing seniority and authority:

- **Coordinators**: Organize on-site interviews, including setting up interview panels and booking conference rooms.

- **Sourcers**: Identify potential candidates using LinkedIn or other specialized tools and do initial outreach (these are the people who send LinkedIn messages). Sourcer performance is measured by how many hires come from candidates they identify.

- **"Recruiters" (per se)**: Owners of the hiring process after initial sourcing. Responsible for most communication with candidates, discussions with managers, attendance at career fairs, salary negotiations, and recruiter presence in hiring committees. Recruiter performance is often measured by number of hires per month and close rate. A common guideline is about three hires per month per recruiter, with one more hire per month generated by having a sourcer.

In my experience, each recruiter usually supports one to two teams, though different arrangements exist. That means that recruiters usually have an incentive to close chiefly for their own team, and they won't necessarily be positioned to route you to the right team for your interests unless you speak up.

Recruiting is a two-sided sales job; recruiters sell a company to a candidate and a candidate to a team, and they make a sale when both sides accept the other.

---

[3]See also: bubble.

What You Need to Know As a Colleague

Engineers and managers evaluate candidates in detail and decide when to make offers; candidates decide for themselves what jobs they'll take; recruiters are the conductors of the whole messy process, accountable for ensuring hires actually happen.

This strong incentive to close candidates is the most important context for engineers; it means that recruiters are almost always the gas, not the brake, in a hiring committee. As an engineer or manager, the encouragement to say yes can be surprising or frustrating, but it is more or less the recruiter's job: to get hires done.

As a colleague, it's been important for me to realize over time that recruiters' jobs are hard and underappreciated. The job is difficult because the recruiter

   A. Is not a technical expert and can only go so far in evaluating the candidate themselves

   B. Needs to work with both sides of the transaction at once

   C. Deals with some of the most notoriously cranky, entitled, and antisocial people (us)

   D. Is subject to many obstacles beyond their control, like the company's salary bands and reputation

Overcoming those challenges requires considerable social skills, energy, and adaptability; the best recruiters I know are astonishingly positive, energetic, and well-organized.

Finally, it's underappreciated because engineers (usually) only appreciate engineering skill and don't respect the difficulty and necessity of recruiting work. In tech companies, recruiters are sometimes considered ancillary to engineers (i.e., lower on the totem pole), but I advise you to start your work with them (as with anyone!) from a position of appreciation and respect for a hard job done well. Now fully understanding this context for the role, let's move on to how to best work with recruiters as a candidate.

What You Need to Know As a Candidate

Since the recruiter's job is to close candidates, the recruiter is usually your ally in the hiring process; therefore, don't agonize about making the perfect impression. Since it's the engineering team's job to evaluate your technical skills, the most important criteria they screen on are background and enthusiasm that are credibly specific to their company, so you'll be just fine if you come to the table with respect, enthusiasm, and something to say about why you're interested in the job. Remember that recruiters act as a layer between managers and candidates and operate with considerable discretion; they can and should accidentally put your resume in the recycling bin if you approach them with disrespect or indifference.

Getting Properly Routed

Since a recruiter usually supports one team, their incentive is to get you hired on that team; they may need explicit feedback to help a candidate with specific interests or a specific technical background get to the right team within a company. This means that if you're routed to a suboptimal team, it's appropriate to be quite vocal (but always friendly and respectful) in expressing your preferences.

Asking Questions

Don't be shy whatsoever; recruiters are usually happy to help out with just about any questions at all. If you need to talk to an engineering manager (a much more critical audience, I'll note), they can connect you with them too.

Levels, Titles, and Compensation at Tech Companies

This section will describe how Silicon Valley-style software companies handle job levels, compensation, and engineering performance. Every firm has its own systems, and you're likely to find more informal practices at smaller companies, but the fundamentals apply quite broadly.

Level and Title

Level is fundamentally an HR concept, one that applies across all disciplines at most large companies: an integer on a role-specific scale, like Data Scientist II or Designer 1. Each level has an associated allowable compensation "band" (allowable range); this observation will come into play in our section on negotiation. Across companies, titles match up imperfectly, but comparisons are often possible (people know that Staff Engineer is higher than Senior Engineer). Companies usually level engineers based on some notion of their "scope," the level of impact they can have on the company's outcomes. It is often, though not always, expected that engineers at higher levels have a capacity for greater leadership, coordination, and architecture work—that they will achieve more impact by leadership and decision-making than by what they personally code.

As a young engineer, you'll wonder: How much does title matter, and why, and what level should I be?

Title matters for two main reasons: your level determines your maximum compensation, and it can help you market yourself as you look for new roles. However, I frequently caution young engineers to avoid excessive preoccupation with title. It emphatically is not its own reward, you may go up and down in title as you move across companies, and, since compensation bands can overlap, increased title doesn't even guarantee greater compensation. I encourage you to focus, by and large, on the forms of compensation you can use every day—money and personal growth.

There's one important caveat—as you advance in your career, you do want to make sure to eventually reach Senior Engineer level, which most would consider the first valid "terminal level"—it's considered acceptable to never advance beyond that title. This is not usually the case for Software Engineer and Software Engineer II, for which there are "up or out" expectations. I've never actually heard of someone being fired for failing to advance beyond those lower levels, but it is expected that you'll be improving and inching toward promotion.

Here's a rough sketch of how it looks at many companies (details, like exact level numbers, will vary). You can check out often-accurate summaries of well-known companies at levels.fyi.

Title	Level	Experience (Years)	Scope	Base Salary
Software Engineer	3	0–3	Do what people tell you	$110,000–$130,000
Software Engineer II	4	2–6	Take on a project, do own project management, and work with others	$120,000–$165,000
Senior Software Engineer	5	4–?	Manage projects with numerous moving pieces, lead others, and set some direction	$160,000–$195,000
Staff Software Engineer	6	8–?	Lead very large projects (or multiple very large projects) and set direction for a large org, almost completely self-directed	$190,000–$230,000
Principal Software Engineer	7	12–?	Set direction for significant part of the entire company	$220,000–$250,000

Compensation

Your compensation in software engineering has three components.

Base Salary

Your base salary shows up every few weeks as long as you're employed; it keeps you sheltered, fed, and clothed. You may get a 2–5% raise annually or 10%+ if you're promoted. I suggest strongly that you treat this as your only compensation for budgeting purposes, since it is far more predictable than the rest of your compensation package.

Bonus

Bonuses usually show up once a year; a multiplier (call it ß) is often calculated based on your performance, then you get ß * salary. 10–20% of is fairly normal, but 0% could happen if you perform poorly, as could 100% if you change the world at the right company.

Equity Compensation Basics

"Equity compensation" means paying you with stock ·(restricted stock units, or "RSUs") or stock options (typically incentive stock options, or "ISOs") in your company. Equity compensation is almost universal in Silicon Valley, but less common in other parts of the world.

You probably know what stock is; stock options are a financial instrument derived from stock, where what you hold is the right to buy stock at a locked-in price (the "strike price"); so, if you hold the right to buy a share at $1, and the price goes to $10, you can "exercise" the option at $1 to buy the share, sell the share at $10, and pocket the difference.

There are two reasons engineers are compensated in equity—the first is to incentivize you to help your company succeed (you want your shares to be worth something) and the second is because stock options can have tax advantages (as well as downsides) over other forms of compensation—a very basic primer on the related tax issues is found below.

Equity compensation is often, but not always, structured as grants that "vest" (become yours) over four years with a one-year "cliff"—the first year's shares vest in bulk at the end of year 1, after which shares vest monthly. For example, you might be granted 4,000 incentive stock options (ISOs) in Acme Software to vest over 4 years (48 months); you'll become the owner of 1000 options (1/4) after 1 year, then another 1/48 every month for the 3 years after that (some companies structure things differently, such as "back-loading" the grant; vesting more in later years).

RSU compensation at a large public company can be highly liquid—once the shares are yours, they're yours, and it's easy as pie to convert them into cash on the public market. Its value can still vary wildly over time, but you can count it as more or less money when you evaluate a package.

Equity in a small private company, however, can be extremely illiquid—there is no public market for it, it expires after some number of years, and you may be contractually forbidden from selling on any private market. Startups often overstate the outlook for their stock—my opinion when evaluating a package is that if it can't be sold today, it should be counted conservatively in your financial planning. Your salary pay will almost certainly go home with you, but your equity in a tiny private company could just as well become nothing as something.

Stock options also often come with a critical encumbrance—if you leave the company, you often have only 30 or 60 days to decide whether to exercise your vested options or let them evaporate into nothing, a decision which can have important tax consequences in the United States.

Equity Compensation Taxation in the United States (Why You Should Consider Exercising Early)

This section is not intended to be comprehensive; instead, it aims only to alert you to a couple of important tax properties of option compensation in the United States. If part of your pay is equity, you would be *extremely* well-advised to consult a tax professional, probably a CPA. It will cost a few hundred dollars, but it may save you infinite headaches in the future.

If you're compensated with RSUs at a public company, they're generally taxed as regular income, and your company will withhold income tax in kind when your grants vest—that is, a percentage will be taken right off the top before you get them. That withholding percentage may not match your actual tax rate, so you should double-check, or you may be surprised by your large tax bill at the end of the year.

If you're compensated in incentive stock options (ISOs), things are a bit more complicated, and I recommend you educate yourself with the well-regarded *Consider Your Options* by Kaye Thomas. I'll highlight two points.

Capital Gains Taxes

If you hold a stock for a long period of time, and the price grows in that time, you may pay capital gains taxes when you sell the shares, instead of higher income taxes. For you, it means that if you are compensated in options and exercise them early (which takes money), and then the company grows in value, you may pay much lower taxes than if you had exercised and sold at the same time.

Alternative Minimum Tax (AMT)

Great, lower taxes! This part is the catch, summarized only at a very high level.

The AMT is a mechanism to ensure that America's taxpayers don't unreasonably avoid paying taxes by fancy footwork—it's a floor on your tax rate, and it applies to ISOs. Stock options have a kind of estimated fair market value (FMV) based on a 409A valuation of a company, and they also have a strike price, what you have to pay to convert your options into shares. The AMT says that if you exercise a stock option, you may owe taxes on FMV minus strike price. If a company's valuation has gone up a lot since your options were granted, that may be an astronomical sum in taxes, but since your shares may not be liquid, you may need to pay out of pocket.

That property matters enormously in at least one specific case—when you want to leave a private company. At that time, you'll likely have to either exercise or abandon your options within two months; you could be—and I have been—faced with a tough choice about staying or abandoning shares you couldn't afford to pay taxes on, all of which together means that if you join a company and your options are extremely cheap, you would do well to consider exercising them before the 409A goes up and makes that expensive or impossible. I will reiterate that professional advice is called for.

Share Salary Information As Much As Possible

Before you set out to evaluate offers and negotiate compensation, you should arm yourself with information about the landscape. What are other people with your skills and experience making in the industry? What are they making at this company?

If you know the landscape, you can answer questions like: Is this a good offer by this company's standards? If not, they probably have room to go higher. Could I get more somewhere else? Armed with those answers, you can get the best offer for yourself by negotiating harder or by simply going to better-paying companies.

Apart from what you may find on sites like levels.fyi, I think there's only one way to acquire that information: sharing as much compensation information with your friends and colleagues as you possibly can. Engineers are squeamish about sharing this information, and employers love that, because it puts all the clarity in their hands at negotiation time. There's no reason to be squeamish. Sharing salary information isn't whatsoever unprofessional. Your employer may try to tell you it is, for the simple reason that they have an advantage if you believe that. You might be worried that you'll be ashamed if it turns out you make less—you might be worried your friends will be resentful if it turns out you do. Sweep away those worries. Whichever of you makes less is about to be fortified with the tools to do better.

Negotiating

When I got my first few job offers, I was nervous about negotiating for better compensation. Did people do that? What would the company think? Would the hiring manager be angry? Would it get me anywhere? What should I say?

Yes, people negotiate on compensation. This section will argue that you should almost always do so. We'll first discuss compensation "bands" and what they imply about your initial offer. Then, we'll talk about the incentives of the parties involved and how you can negotiate effectively without harming your eventual employment relationship.

At large tech companies, a recruiter or committee (sometimes a manager) will compose an offer package based on guidelines called "bands" for a given level, your interview performance, your current compensation, and your competing offers. For example, it might look like this (exact numbers are only for illustration and are probably already wildly wrong at the time you read this):

Title	Level	Experience	Salary	Equity Grant (Shares)
SWE	3	0–3 years	$110,000–$130,000	5,000–8,000
SWE II	4	2–6 years	$120,000–$165,000	7,500–10,000
Senior SWE	5	5–? years	$160,000–$195,000	9,500–15,000
Staff SWE	6	8–? years	$190,000–$230,000	15,000–20,000
Principal SWE	7	12–?	$220,000–$250,000	18,000–25,000

Level is set by experience and interview performance. Most likely, your initial offer will not be "top of band," and most of the time, if they like you enough to give you an offer, they like you enough to move closer to the top of the range, though going beyond the top of the band (i.e., up a level) may be hard or impossible. In general, there's very likely money available for the taking, and you should always try to take it.

Let's take a moment to understand the incentives of the people involved. The recruiter always has the strongest incentive to get you to accept, because they're compensated based on their hire rates and they don't care one bit about the cost (the cost of hires isn't usually held against them). The manager is in a similar boat—they need to hire, and the money doesn't typically come out of their personal budget, so they just want to get you the best offer they can. However, there's usually some bureaucrat, director, or committee that needs to sign off on the package, which means that you need to arm the recruiter and manager with a justification for improving the offer. The best ammunition you can give them is another package to point to, either your current compensation or a competing offer.

The most powerful leverage you can have is better current compensation; companies may do their best to match whatever you make today, often exactly to the dime. Therefore, you should feel free to say, "my current compensation is X, and I would like to see that matched to accept this offer." The second best leverage is a better competing offer—it both signals your quality in general and gives the recruiter and manager something specific to point to. Even if you don't have a slam-dunk better package elsewhere, your negotiating strategy should probably still be based on some dimension where the alternative wins—for example, if your current company has a better bonus program or another company's equity is more liquid (e.g., they're already public).[4]

Negotiating with a respectful and positive attitude usually won't harm your eventual relationship with your manager (not without exception obviously—smaller companies can take things more personally). The negotiation will usually take place through the recruiter, who will keep the manager informed throughout. Asking for more usually feels crass to engineers, but it's just business for the recruiter, who deals with compensation packages all day long. You should negotiate unapologetically and professionally[5]; remember that negotiating is completely reasonable and that if you stay positive and businesslike, they will too. Especially, you should never get offended or complain; this is business between adults.

---

[4]This may change as you become more experienced—if you're very senior, your strategy may focus on the value you're confident you can deliver.

[5]You're well-advised to take the same approach in any in-house negotiations too!

I'd emphasize my enthusiasm about a company (which should be genuine); that positivity encourages your manager and recruiter to see that if they come through for you, there's a good chance you'll accept. It also serves to ensure that feelings are positive when the time comes for you to start. Here are a few example lines to try out:

- The team really impressed me, and I'm excited about the product. My offer at SmartSoft has a base salary of $150k and a similar equity package; can you match them on the base salary?

- Thanks for your quick reply. I really enjoyed my interviews, and the team was really friendly. The base salary looks good to me, but my current package has a 20% bonus target, and Acme Startup doesn't have a bonus program. Can you balance that out with a bump in the equity or base salary?

I suggest the convention of expressing what you want once, firmly, and if they say no, taking that as their final offer to weigh against competitors.

Learning and Growing

Congratulations: You've finished your training, landed your first software job, and started your journey as a professional. Your growth, though, is just getting started. Some engineers carry around a specific dream, like solving a problem they loathe or helping a community they love. Absent that, or assuming good work at a software company is part of your vision, I'll offer you a placeholder goal: to solve the biggest problems your abilities allow, constantly challenging yourself and nurturing your technical and people skills. While other chapters discuss many of those skills in detail, this chapter will focus on the trajectory per se, including self-study and mentorship, while also discussing how companies evaluate performance.

Read Every Day: The Practice of Study

You should be reading (or watching or listening to) technical content every single weekday. People say all the time that they'd rather hire someone smart than someone who "just knows a bunch of stuff"; I happen to disagree. The best engineers I've worked with know tons of cold hard facts, much of it from self-study. You'll discover your own study rhythm, but your default position should be to study every single week, ideally every weekday; it should be built into your routine like physical exercise or time with friends. My personal

D. Heller, *Building a Career in Software*, https://doi.org/10.1007/978-1-4842-6147-7_3

method is to dedicate every morning commute to technical reading, but I've also known people who read every day after breakfast or take a larger block every weekend at a coffee shop.

We read to acquire three things:

- Facts we can use tactically in our day-to-day jobs, like optimizations, libraries, or tools we didn't know about

- Fundamental concepts we can use to design systems and drive projects, like design patterns, algorithms, project management methodologies, and reliability techniques

- A sense of the landscape of the field's technologies, so we're prepared to choose among them

What you read is specific to your job and interests, but here's my menu:

- **Technical white papers**: Those from academia or companies like Google and Facebook can offer theoretical insight, though they're generally the least directly practical reading.

- **Conferences**: Are a good way to get a broad, practical sense of what's going on in the industry; except when you have a specific need to network in a domain, their main purpose is to carve out more time than you otherwise have for study (after all, the talks are usually online too). They are often expensive, and quality varies; definitely see if your company can send you to one a year!

- **Newsletters and blog posts**: Are a good way to find a steady flow of bite-sized practical updates. I tend to read these with at least one of my reading days per week.

- **Books**: I like to read technical books cover to cover on subjects like databases, build systems, and programming languages. They often don't offer the best density, but I find reading a whole book cover to cover the best way to get the sense of the whole landscape for a technology—so I can start using it without a constant worry that I'm missing the obvious.

- **Reading code**: Reveals the real patterns and technologies used in successful (or unsuccessful) projects; the best engineers I know read a lot of code, which helps them build a bigger toolbox and stronger opinions about design and style. Well-known open-source projects can be a good place to start, but their quality varies! Ask a senior colleague for a suggestion in your team's language.

- **Online courses**: The quality of courses available for free online is breathtaking; if you're breaking into a brand new technical area and need an overview, this is your best bet.

- **Podcasts**: The last five years have seen an explosion in quality technical podcasts, often offering deep discussions of real systems at successful companies. This should be your go-to if you drive to work.

- **Discretionary coding**: It lets you really use the systems you've read about. It demands creativity I almost entirely lack, but it's the only way to fully learn a language or demystify a framework outside of the office; you can solve a problem for yourself or make a contribution to an open-source project.

I struggle to balance all these content types. If you only read papers, you're too theoretical; if you only read open source code, you'll struggle to bootstrap the big picture; if you only listen to podcasts, you don't challenge yourself enough to understand theory the way a paper challenges you. I don't have a schedule to offer. Personally, my scheduling is ad hoc except when I have a specific technical goal. I read every morning; I catch up on newsletters at least once a week (usually Friday), I read a book when I feel like I haven't "in a while," and when I finish a book, I read a few papers and listen to a few podcasts; when something interesting comes up at work or from a friend, I read something specific at interrupt priority. I wouldn't sweat the schedule too much as long as you're learning and erring toward content relevant to your work.

Mentorship

Finding a Mentor

A great mentor is a wonderful asset, in every respect similar to a pet unicorn. Your expectation should be that mentors of any kind are hard to find, and good mentors ten times as hard, which means that you should never look to mentorship to be the engine of your growth—you should expect to teach yourself. I see countless young people lament that their careers can't move forward because they can't find a mentor; I think their careers aren't moving forward because they labor under the delusion that anything other than constant self-directed study and effort produce advancement. Even if you do happen to find a mentor, you remain the owner of your growth (refer to "If You Only Take Away One Thing" in Chapter 1).

However, if you encounter someone you admire that you think might have something to teach you, you should feel free to seek out their advice—in my opinion, asking a more senior person for mentorship is perfectly reasonable.

As Sheryl Sandberg noted in *Lean In*, to ask for mentorship as a passive receptacle of knowledge ("here I am, mentor me!") is not a persuasive way to engage a busy, results-driven person. When you reach out for mentorship, you should ideally come with a specific issue to ask about and perhaps a concrete proposal for an ongoing relationship. If you're lucky, your mentor will have their own rich theory of mentorship, but if not, you can start with the following:

- **Explain your goals**: Maybe you want to level up your project management, maybe you want to master some new technologies, or maybe you just want to get promoted (not the most compelling goal, but it's something).

- **Suggest that you meet every 2 weeks for 30 minutes**: Once a week is too much of an imposition; once a month is too little to build a rapport. An hour is actually optimal, but asking for an hour of a busy person's time is a strong move; start with 30 minutes, and you can ask to double that once you've gotten to know each other. Propose that

    - You will come prepared every time to discuss areas you particularly want to grow, and your mentor will share their thoughts and assign reading in those areas.

    - You will come every time with at least two specific questions to ask.

    - You'll bring proposals/documents/emails for your mentor to review with you.

Making the Most of Your Mentor

If you've had the good luck to lock in a mentor, you should be constantly thinking about how to make the most of the relationship. Here's how I'd start:

- Think about ways you want to improve; come to every 1:1 ready to discuss them.

- Prepare for meetings by thinking about recent challenges; always come with at least two recent struggles to discuss, like a meeting that went poorly, a proposal that you're struggling with, or an idea you're struggling to evangelize. Come to the meeting with notes; discuss what happened, what you want to achieve, and what you'd like them to advise you about.

- Maintain a shared 1:1 agenda, and always update that document in advance; it shows your commitment to making the most of the relationship and helps organize the conversation.

- Think hard about your own aspirations to prepare for goal setting.

- Follow through religiously on any reading suggested by your mentor, and come with questions.

- Review the mentoring techniques from *Chapter 8*; when you feel that you're not getting the most out of your 1:1s, suggest that you try some of those techniques together. If you run out of steam, get on that Internet and search for exercises others find useful.

If you feel you're not getting enough from your mentor, think first of stepping up your mentee game; you're an empowered professional trying to learn from a busy colleague, and it's up to you to make the most of it.

Imposter Syndrome Is Underrated

A lot of talk on blogs and LinkedIn goes into overcoming imposter syndrome. I say embrace self-skepticism and doubt yourself every day. In a fast-moving industry where lots of your knowledge expires every year, even the most junior people around you constantly cook up skills you don't have; you stay competitive by applying yourself with the determination (and even fear) of the novice. The upside of this treadmill is that every engineer is on it: just because you're an imposter doesn't mean that other people are more deserving than you, because they're imposters too. You should advocate for yourself, take risks, pat yourself on the back when things go well, and, as you start to build a track record of solving problems, trust your skills and adaptability. Just make no mistake: you're only as good as the last problem you solve.

Having Your Own Project Ideas

Sometimes we're handed amazing projects; it's convenient and it's fun. At some point in your career, though, you won't need that; in your final form, you'll look around you, see need or opportunity, propose projects, and lead them to fruition. In fact, this is a good indicator of whether you're ready for the big leagues; if you find yourself saying, "my manager isn't giving me the project I need to get my Staff Engineer promotion," then you'll know you aren't ready, because an expert finds their own work.

How, though?

There are two options. The first is to be brilliant—to conceive of projects by sheer creativity and insight. I've never done this in my life, but if you can, you'll go far.

The second option, the people's creativity, is knowledge. Diligent students don't need brilliance to generate good projects; they learn and learn and learn, then diff their knowledge of the state of the art against the state of their neighborhood. If you don't have good ideas yet: keep learning. Read papers and watch talks: somewhere out there, someone is writing about technology they've built that works better than yours. If you find the right paper, you'll find your opportunities. Ask your manager, your customers, and your teammates what they think is broken and what opportunities aren't being exploited; maybe they'll put you onto something great.

Thus, read every day, and don't worry if your ideas aren't brilliant; I've never had a brilliant thought in my life, but that doesn't stop me from solving the occasional problem.

Performance Reviews

Personal growth is the foundation of career growth, but at least once a year, your employer is going to try to reach its own conclusions about your performance; that process has financial and career consequences, and it can often loom large in the work year. This section will describe the performance review processes companies use to allocate promotions and raises and will prepare you to put your best foot forward.

Every company has systems to incentivize employees. These systems distribute finite money and promotions[1] among employees to create the best performance the system can achieve as the leaders of the company perceive it.[2]

Leaders may have wildly different ideas about the behavior they want to encourage and the properties they care about in a compensation system. Some leaders believe in comfort and earnest collaboration; others believe that anxiety and competition inspire excellence. Some think mostly equal compensation creates a productive familial atmosphere, while others think a winner-take-all system is more motivating. Despite these differences of temperament, these systems usually work roughly the same way, with modest differences in the details.

---

[1]Finite because promotions determine compensation.
[2]In principle higher compensation and greater authority need not be coupled, but in practice they are.

The process starts with executives and the board allocating a pool of money and equity for raises and bonuses across each division in the company; that pool is further subdivided down the org tree.

It continues with self-reviews (covered in the next section) and peer feedback, where everyone in the organization receives feedback from three to five peers. This feedback process has two purposes: the first is usually a genuine desire for individuals to learn from each other, and the second is to inform managers of how their people are doing as an input to the performance process. In my experience, there's variation in the degree of openness in this peer process—at some companies, the equilibrium is for no one to give substantial negative feedback, whereas at others, there's a genuine cultural commitment to openness. Your mileage may vary; ask an experienced colleague.

After or concurrent to the peer review process, the money-focused process begins in earnest with battle royale-style meetings of managers, often called calibration, to "stack rank" their employees, creating a ranking from best to worst of the employees at every level. Some companies claim not to stank rank, but that's a lie—whether there's a spreadsheet with a sorted list or not, there exists a total order on compensation, so there is a stack rank in practice. This ranking is fed up the chain for consistency checks and eventually determines compensation. The curve of compensation with respect to ranking can vary: maybe the top employee gets 1.5x the median employee, or maybe they get 100x. Managers usually want more compensation for their own people at the expense of other teams, so the battle royale can get pretty heated; remember that if your manager didn't come through for you, it's more likely that they couldn't than that they didn't want to.

After an arduous bureaucratic checking process, engineers receive their reviews in person from their managers. This review usually has two to three parts:

- A compensation package including some or all of cash bonus, cash raise, and equity.

- A written review structured around a rubric of areas like coding, architecture, and leadership. This review usually has a loose relationship to the actual money, being written after the money-oriented process is concluded.

- A promotion (or not).

I want to end this section with some advice about your emotional approach to this review: to the extent possible, don't take it personally, and accept the feedback with all the grace you can summon. You might disagree, you might get fed up with your compensation and go elsewhere, you might be enraged with your manager's misunderstanding of your efforts, but in the end, it's just a way for an organization to allocate its finite resources, and your manager is a human with an imperfect grasp of the fractal achievements and failings of their team.

Chapter 6 will cover two closely related problems: accepting feedback and collaborating with your boss, including upward communication, advocating for yourself, and handling grievances.

Self-reviews

Many performance processes require an annual or semiannual self-review, where you summarize your work and its impact, essentially making argument (not in so many words) that you should get a good review and a good bonus.

The overall content is the review is pretty easy—it comes from what you've done, and if you're smart, you'll have documented that work prodigiously in a Worklog (Chapter 5). I'll offer a few tips to optimize your self-review.

First, it should not just be a list of tasks; like any piece of writing, you need to construct a narrative that your reader can follow. That means, not "I completed tasks CODE-1001, CODE-1002, CODE-1003…" but "I managed the inbound bug queue for the store page, including working with stakeholders to prioritize bugs and fixing over 20 bugs."

This carries us into our second point: your narrative should emphasize not just your productivity (which is obviously important) but your leadership, autonomy, and impact, which are the essential qualities of "senior" engineers, prized by managers and committees. Points to emphasize might include where you

- Led meetings
- Did your own project management
- Proposed new projects
- Took the initiative to improve infrastructure
- Owned a component, especially managing inbound requests, supporting stakeholders, reviewing code for other teams, etc.
- Mentored more junior colleagues
- Provided design feedback

Finally, your self-review is an opportunity to be your own advocate; if you've messed up, you should never conceal it, but this isn't the place to enumerate your mistakes. If you're obliged to mention where you've failed, the answer should, more or less, take the form: I should have led more, I should have taken more initiative, I should have seen the big picture more, that is, aspirations to the next level of execution.

Stop Worrying About Title

Most young people I meet these days are chronically obsessed with getting promoted. I argue: that's mostly misplaced. Title is a bureaucratic blessing, the product of a committee of committees, and a poor way to measure your career success. First, because you need your own sense of the meaning of achievement, you must, as you mature, evaluate your work for yourself. Second, because we have the good fortune to build things for a living, skill and achievement create opportunity and fulfillment in the long term.

My experience personally, and observation of my peers, is that advancement and fulfillment flow from constantly hunting the toughest, most interesting problems you can find and solving them for the sheer joy of building things (what is engineering if not that?); preoccupation with promotion, in my experience, is an obstacle to it, because it keeps you from bringing your best effort to your core responsibilities.

That's not to say that you shouldn't proactively get the best deal for yourself; you should, because money, unlike a bureaucratic badge, comes home with you to buy things you like. But, if you're spending your time worrying about whether a committee wants to put a feather in your cap, you're missing the point of your career.

Changes

Changing companies, teams, and projects is one of the most stressful parts of life in a fast-changing industry, especially for a new arrival to the business world. At the very minimum, you'll make one big change in your career: starting your first job. Right after that, you're pretty well guaranteed to start asking yourself tough questions. Am I ramping up fast enough? When should I make the move? How can I make the transition clean? What does it mean that I'm in a rut? This chapter will discuss all these challenges of professional transition.

On Fear, Confusion, and Self-Loathing: Starting New Jobs

For six months after I started my first job, I was well and truly sure every day that today someone would finally figure out that I didn't know anything and summarily terminate me. That is not in the least an exaggeration; I had trouble sleeping, I had visions of future destitution (so far not realized), and I was afraid to tell anyone. Around eight months in, I got to chatting with a colleague who had about a year of tenure on me; he said that he'd felt the exact same thing for the first six months. Many people have told me the same since, including some luminaries who've reviewed this book.

Six years later, I started my second job; I had almost the same experience. And a year later, the same. In no case was I, in fact, summarily terminated for incompetence.

© Daniel Heller 2020

D. Heller, *Building a Career in Software*, https://doi.org/10.1007/978-1-4842-6147-7_4

All of the above helped me realize that starting a new engineering job is almost always profoundly unsettling. Even in the rare case where you're brought in as a specialist to do exactly what you do best, you're walking into a labyrinth of Byzantine development flows, barbarous shell scripts, and missing wikis that blunt technical knowledge—and the comfort you knew as an expert in your old job (or school) is out the window.

So, tl;dr: don't worry! Because everyone feels that confusion and unease, no (sensible) veterans expect you to know anything, and you certainly will get better. You should expect six months of struggle to arrive at something resembling ease.

Onboarding in Practice

Companies vary wildly in how much they support new hires. I've heard rumors that there are companies out there where junior people are paired with a supportive senior person who takes a genuine interest in their development and works hard to nurture insight and expertise. I've seen it happen on a few occasions; I flatter myself that as a manager, I even did it once or twice. However, my personal experience has virtually always been that I've been tossed into the fire with no support of any kind, and you should expect that to be your experience too. This is, in some sense, a pity, but you'll be fine, as generations of engineers have.

What you shouldn't do: whine about not having a mentor or anything else (neither did anyone else), panic, or quit.

What you should do: refuse to stay blocked (people will notice), read as much code as you can (it's a good way to learn a system), ask questions as carefully as you can (Chapter 14), take the initiative to befriend your colleagues (suggest tea or coffee), take on dirty tasks and debug relentlessly (it's the best way to learn a system), earn your colleagues' respect with hard work and helpfulness, and be patient. If you're lucky enough to have a proper mentor, think hard about the best way to use them (see "Mentorship" in Chapter 3) . Overall, onboarding is an exercise in hard work, patience, and improvisation—in time, you'll find your way.

When to Change Jobs

Both of my parents repeatedly worked the same jobs for periods of 15 and 20 years; I've already changed roles as many times as they did in their whole careers. In software today, changing jobs every two years isn't too unusual; four years is a generous stay, and a one-year stint is no problem at all on a resume (two or three one-year stints in a row may be a red flag).

The allure of engineering is precisely its constant learning and discovery, which means engineers usually crave novelty. Also, because our field changes constantly, we often keep moving whether we crave it or not; a complacent engineer is an obsolete engineer.

So, I reevaluate my situation every six months, and you should too. If you only consider a move every two years, you're apt to waste too much time; if you consider it every week, you'll always be agonizing and never focusing. So, my cadence is every six months. My mental model is that every 6 months or year (or 18 months; the tours get longer as your projects get bigger), I sign up for a "tour of duty"—I commit to myself and to a manager that I will help them achieve some goal, and I go execute on that without a thought to leaving. When the dust starts to settle, I pop my head back up and ask, is it time to make moves?

There are a million dimensions to a good or bad job, from technology to teammates to commute, so I can't give you any simple algorithm for deciding when it's time to make moves. However, I can offer a few heuristics that have felt right to me.

The first and foremost heuristic is: if you feel a powerful urge to go, and that urge lasts 2–3 months, you should go; when it's time, it's time. That's the easy case! Unfortunately, it isn't the common case; more usually you'll feel a real conflict, you'll love the people but hate the work, love the technology but hate the manager, etc., etc., etc.

If it seems like the interesting work on your team is done and it is converging on maintenance and small tweaks, it may be time to go. You can stay through one more planning cycle to find out; if three to six months pass, and no one can tell you about a plan that sounds impactful, it is time to go.

Momentary struggle isn't a reason to quit; the fun and frustration of every job wax and wane, and tough projects wrap up. However, if you really hate coming to work, it is probably time to go; if you go to bed on Sunday dreading waking up on Monday, and that feeling lasts 3 months, it's time to improve your life

You should keep track of your compensation relative to your peers on that same six-month cadence; if you're way behind your market wage, make no mistake, you should go get your money. You can start by negotiating if you like, but there's no shame in taking a big raise at a new job. Similarly, you can sometimes extract a title bump as part of a move—smaller companies are especially likely to inflate titles as a kind of compensation. I personally value that prize minimally for its own sake (see "Stop Worrying About Title" in Chapter 3), but you may consider it if you believe you're pathologically held back in your current firm, especially from promotion to a terminal role like Senior Engineer.

Finally, if you feel like you aren't learning, it may be time to go. Of course, not every project is a chance to learn—a good engineer will take one for the team now and again to ship software that needs shipping. However, if you've been on the bored bus for three months, and you don't see any prospect for improvement, it's time to go find a new challenge.

How to Change Jobs: Going Out in Style

There's only one way to leave a job: gracefully, gratefully, leaving only beautiful documentation and neatly tied loose ends in your wake.

That's… pretty tough to do. I've almost always gone through two phases when I leave a role or company. First, "I'm going to go out better than anyone has ever gone out"—determination to be your best self and be remembered as a legend. Second, a devastating drop in motivation, making it impossible to do almost anything; that's also when I start to feel all the resentments and frustrations of this phase in my life swelling in me, leaving me with a sour urge to give everyone a piece of my mind.

That second phase is a real bear. I once saw someone crank out beautiful bugfixes and documentation until 10 PM on his last day, but you can set your sights a little lower; a departure with good documentation, reasonable productivity up to the end, no loose ends, and no complaining will be just fine for your reputation.

What you should aim for, realistically, is

- **Most importantly**: Not complaining (to anyone), not bringing others down, and not insulting anyone. The close to part of your career is a natural time to feel strong emotions that will settle with time and perspective; letting them boil over is a great way to burn bridges. Smile, breathe, find your gratitude, and give your notice. Quitting is a natural part of professional life, and it can be done directly and unapologetically—say that you're leaving, and thank your boss for everything they've done for you.

- **Giving at least two full weeks' notice, not including vacation**: More than that is at your discretion, and your employer usually can't demand it (of course, laws and customs vary by location). Two full weeks of time in the office makes sure your team has ample time to learn what they need to from you.

- **As a top priority**: Documenting every single thing that only you know; see "Bus Factor > 1" in Chapter 20. When I've hit my exit documentation out of the park, people have reached out to me repeatedly to thank me, and they'll thank you too.

- **As a secondary priority**: Cleaning up tech debt or key bugs that you're uniquely positioned to fix; fixing a tool or making a nice performance optimization can be a good parting gift to your colleagues.

Maintenance Is for Suckers: Choosing Teams and Projects

Maintenance isn't really for suckers; it's an honorable responsibility as well as the only way to master the difference between what looks good in a blog post and what works in a production system. But I want your full attention for an important point: make the moves you need to make to find good projects, and don't languish in a role where there's nothing interesting left to do.

When choosing projects, you're optimizing for three things: learning, resume/advancement, and satisfaction. Balancing these objectives requires a regular explore–exploit cycle over time. If you're always doing something brand new to you, you're always struggling with the strain of being a novice and never solving the biggest problems available—which means that you're never putting a big achievement on your resume or enjoying the satisfaction of building something grand. On the other hand, if you stay in the exact same space for ten years, your marginal learning will asymptotically approach zero.

As for whether you should work on back-end systems, mobile, or web, machine learning or ads, search or reliability, etc., etc., etc., I can't tell you—times change fast, so ask people you respect what they think is growing (they won't know either—if they did, they would use it to play the stock market, but it's a start). Conditional on having chosen an area of focus, I can offer some simple guidelines.

Someday, you'll be deep and bold enough to have your own vision for teams and companies; I look forward to it. Until then, look for an important problem that needs solving, for a team with a mission that resonates, and for a manager who can convey a concrete desired change in the world and a path to realizing it. That change might be of modest scope (e.g., your company's developers will be able to move faster), but you should understand what needs to change, care about the result, and believe that you'll have to build something big to achieve it.

Most of the work done in the universe of software engineering goes to maintaining and modestly enhancing existing systems in streams of small features and bugs. In my opinion, making that your whole job is for suckers, and you should almost never choose to work on a team where the technology is so mature, and the vision so anemic, that your life is organized around a bug queue rather than a story. The fun, the excitement, the variety, the wind in your hair, and the jewels on a resume come from tackling big, coherent challenges. That doesn't just mean building things from scratch—you might fix performance problems, might improve reliability by fixing a backlog of bugs, might implement a new product vision in existing systems, etc., etc., but until you're ready to retire in place, your job shouldn't be just to manage an endless stream of isolated tiny tweaks. My advice: seek out the biggest, most impactful problems you can find, deliver impact, maintain what you've built long enough to unambiguously prove success, and clean up any messes you've created. Finally, evaluate whether there's a new vision to tackle; if all that's left is repeatedly repainting the house, move on; leave what you've built in superb condition for others to maintain.

I've worried about writing what I just wrote; the world needs its systems maintained, cynicism and selfishness are already a big enough epidemic, and a good career doesn't come from shirking responsibility—you need to do what you're asked to do, solve problems thoroughly, and reason about what really matters for your team and company, not build things just because you want to pad your resume. However, I can't lie: I believe that when what matters on your team becomes permanently boring, it's time to go to a team where what matters is interesting.

The Transition to Management

Sooner or later, you're going to think about making the jump to management. If there's a deeper subject, I haven't found it, and it's a subject treated in countless books, some of them even good books.[1] This book has no manual for management, but I will offer some thoughts on that transition: what the job looks like, its challenges, and considerations for making or not making the move.

Programmers do real stuff; they write code, they operate systems, and they debug outages. Their days are spent building technology. They enjoy a wonderfully crisp feedback loop; every day, an engineer can type on a keyboard, produce code, see it work, and get a sizzling little dopamine shot to let them know they're living right. Much of their impact is based on the code they write with their own hands; as they get more senior, it may be by the power of their ideas and persuasion.

---

[1]Among the best-regarded are *The Manager's Path*, *The Effective Executive*, and *Managing Humans*.

Managers do almost everything through the efforts of others. Their daily problems are nurturing humans, organizing projects, and managing themselves. They send status reports, soothe the anxious, write roadmaps, scold the wrongheaded, review spreadsheets and bugs, and on and on; they hide their emotions to create an atmosphere of positivity. They virtually never do something and feel a sizzling little anything; their life is maintenance, hygiene, nudging their teams in the right direction, and waiting anxiously for their engineers to deliver. The relationship between their efforts and their outcomes is much more abstract and slippery, which means that the transition is almost always accompanied by an identity crisis—a struggle to accept life with less direct impact. However, managers have, to a point, authority. Their job is to be accountable for a team, and so they have automatic leverage beyond themselves, the kind of leverage individual contributors may or may not achieve through reason and persuasion. They can decide on roadmap; they're apt to make consequential calls.

You might consider being a manager if

- You love people.

- You're naturally patient and don't mind difficult collaborations; you're emotionally steady.

- You don't mind meetings.

- You're a good communicator and project manager.

- You're chaffing at the limits of what you can do as an IC and looking for more leverage.

You might consider passing on this one if

- You're introverted; you hate meetings. Popular opinion now holds that introversion shouldn't be a disability for management, but I politely disagree from my own experience; you are going to have to spend a lot of time with others.

- You have trouble managing your emotions or struggle with difficult social situations.

- You really, really adore coding and can't see living without it.

I was squarely in the middle; I love people, I'm a decent project manager and communicator, and I was hungry for more scope. For me, being a manager was a wonderful learning experience, about teams, companies, and myself. It pulled the curtain back on bureaucracy and set the record straight on where the capable grown-ups are (nowhere); it exposed me to a much bigger variety of technology and people than I'd had the pleasure to know before; and I did feel a real thrill at seeing a large organization move, feeling that I had set it in motion.

On the other hand, I would have meetings 6 to 10 hours a day, and almost every moment of every meeting, I was dying to escape; I simply can't be in a conference room that much. I found the wait for others to execute extremely frustrating, and I was hungry to just do things on my own. And I was aesthetically troubled by the need to conceal my anxieties and frustrations so completely (which, to be clear, I believe to be the right thing to do; see "Harmony" in Chapter 8).

You'll have to decide which half of that story sounds more like you.

Adaptability Is Everything

I started working at Apple in July 2007, which was just after the release of the iPhone but just before it became arguably the most successful product of the twenty-first century. Apple had already existed for around 30 years, and in the software organization, the Mac had been the big deal prior to the arrival of the phone. As the iPhone rose, I watched some engineers go through a painful transition—experts on the Mac software stack, proud and occasionally territorial, gradually became less relevant as iPhone sales soared. I saw two types of responses: the people who saw that times had changed and remade themselves for an iPhone-first world and a minority who clung to the old turf, saying "no" to requests from the iPhone team and gradually becoming less relevant. History has made it pretty clear that adapting to the iPhone was the right move, and clinging to Mac territory, not so much. I learned a lesson watching all that happen in slow motion—adaptability is everything. As technology and business landscapes change, you'll face frequent choices between exploiting your expertise and status in a previous wave area and giving those things up status to struggle painfully in a new area.

That explore–exploit trade-off is far from simple. If you're constantly changing teams or companies, you're never building up enough momentum making big contributions (or, maybe, big money); if you're always sitting still, your learning will gradually trend to zero. A willingness to struggle and change also doesn't guarantee anything—you can bet on the wrong technology or just become a victim of industry ageism. The promise I made myself was that I'd never go down clinging to the old ways when things had already changed or become one of the people with tons of experience that can't execute because they don't think they have to keep learning and struggling. The need to keep struggling can be a bitter pill—as you put more projects behind you, you want to be able to slow down and enjoy the fruits of your learning, and perhaps we can now and then. However, we chose engineering for the joy of learning and figuring things out, and in a field that's essentially about change, where your expertise in one technology can be obsoleted quickly by the advent of another, we survive by changing ourselves.

Burnout, Bouncing Back, and Balance

I was once so burned out that when my boss asked me to send a simple email, I sat down at my laptop and couldn't bring myself to type a single word; there were several weeks where I'm not sure I did a single hour's real work, though I showed up at the office, sat at my laptop, and tried to will my brain to do something useful. I thought that my career was literally over, that I would have to leave software and find a brand new career if I wanted to keep a roof over my head. As it happened, my career wasn't over, and I bounced back to write a few more lines of code. This section will discuss work–life balance, the nature and causes of burnout, and my personal thoughts on how we can recover. It's based entirely on my own anecdotal experience; for science, you'll have to look somewhere else. Still, I think my observations have occasionally been helpful to colleagues.

The Model

Burnout is the conditioned sense that work is much more painful than it is rewarding so that we come to shy away from it—when stress dominates the rewards of work for long enough that we're trained to avoid work and only enormous effort can dominate our instinct to get the heck out of there.

I think the equation is as easy to understand as it is hard to apply. All work has rewards and stresses; people have some blend of motivations and some level of resilience to stresses. Avoiding burnout means (a) trying to keep our job rewards stronger than our stressors and (b) refreshing our resilience in our personal lives.

Ideal work is

1. **Just hard enough**: It offers the satisfaction of overcoming challenges with your unique skills, with neither exhaustive struggle nor excessive ease.

2. **Profitable**: So you have security and comfort.

3. **Educational and varied**: So you feel that you're growing and investing in your future.

4. **Impactful**: So you care about the outcome of your work.

5. **Reasonably comfortable**: So you don't suffer from physical discomfort, emotional abuse, social isolation, or surrealist bureaucratic torture every day.

6. **Reasonably social**: So you feel a warmth of human connection with your colleagues.

Those rewards are our motivation, the fuel keeping the airplane in the air.

Their inverses are struggle, the grind—stresses like fear of failure, discomfort, financial worry, repetitiveness, futility, and isolation.

Resilience is how intensely we feel those stresses (and, perhaps, how much we can enjoy those rewards)—our reservoir of mental strength and capacity for pleasure. We refill this with both enjoyment at work and refreshment in our free time; the less pleasurable our work, the more important it is to revive ourselves outside.

So, much as you probably figured, if your ratio of reward to struggle is bad enough for long enough, your animal brain will learn to avoid work, and you'll have to struggle to squeeze effort out of yourself. And, pretty much like you figured, a rich life outside of work pushes back against that process. So, our goals are to make our work rewarding, manage our level of struggle, and defend the sources of refreshment in the rest of our lives.

Struggle Is Constant

Struggle is a constant; as you grow, you just struggle with bigger problems. First it's to make a single bugfix, then a good program, then a large system, then to lead the efforts of a group, then to have your own grand vision, then to scale that vision to a large, imperfect organization or company, and so on, with the risks of failure growing proportional to our scope. This invariant means that avoiding struggle isn't a goal—our goals are first to ensure that our struggles are productive (stemming from the difficulty of our goals, not the bugs in our setup), and second to manage the stress of that struggle.

Protecting a Corner of Your Life

Someone once gave me the advice of deciding how many hours per week I was willing to work, drawing a line, and holding it. I'm terrible at this, but I agree with it, and the people I know who do draw such a line seem, if anything, more successful than the workaholics. To paraphrase *The Effective Executive*, as a knowledge worker, there's always more to do than can possibly be done; ruthless prioritization is necessary for any success, so we should cultivate it and use it to draw our line. When I came back from burnout, my first, tentative line was—no work on Saturdays, and no work after 10 PM except in emergencies.

I've learned to make a constant, mindful practice of defending a corner of my life from work and filling it with both hobbies and friendship, even when I'm excited about work. On the one hand, it will replenish your resilience to adversity. On the second hand, if you do find yourself unbearably weary at work, it will prevent a sense that your life has become empty. This habit comes easily to some people, not to me. The importance of a joyful social life and strong relationships is both obvious and beyond this book's scope, other than to say that friendship and partnership nourish most people. I will, however, venture to advise you to get and keep, as soon as you can:

(a) A hobby you can find at least five minutes a day for

(b) A whole day per week that you absolutely will not work, no matter what

My own experience is that burnout can sneak up on you, and when it does, you can be surprised by how gradually and thoroughly work has expanded to fill your life. That single-mindedness can be exhilarating, but if and when it turns sour, you can feel that your life is hollow and wobbly. The only remedy I know to offer are diligence in nurturing a counterweight of pleasure and satisfaction that work can't touch.

Not Giving a Hoot

The smallest consequence of failure in software is wasted time, that is, opportunity cost; generally, though, the more valuable work is, the higher the stakes of failure, whether financial, personal, or existential (shout-out to everyone working on global warming and medical devices). I think that means that scaling our impact requires us to gradually accept higher stakes of failure and find comfort with that responsibility; I personally meditate to try to overcome my intense natural risk aversion. I'm not suggesting you quit your job right away to found a self-funded startup; we should strive to take the highest expected value risks we can. But we should try to accept that as we grow, we need to take on more grave and lonelier responsibilities and try not to care too much.

Bouncing Back

Bouncing back is possible, even when you feel that you can't type a single keystroke more; I think that knowledge alone has been comforting to the people I've seen in the worst state of burnout. It may happen on its own, or it may require a radical change of circumstances—I recommend the latter—but it can happen. Don't give up! Change your job, find a hobby, and be patient—in my case it took about six months to come back from feeling totally useless to feeling strong and eager, but I came all the way back, tougher than before.

My Experience

I had joined a company after a change in my technical focus, was way behind everyone else technically, and put the pedal to the metal to catch up. Before long, I was working literally seven days a week and making progress. A year of seven-day weeks later, I was a manager, managing three teams several time zones apart. While I had one good manager working under me, I had tried and failed to hire any managers in Europe to further partition the work; I had 16 people reporting to me directly. I had allowed my calendar to bloat with meetings until it was jammed from 6 AM or 7 AM to 5 PM with only an hour or two of being meeting-free in between; I would start my "real work" in the evening. The organization was also complicated and stressful; my team's mission overlapped completely with a sibling team's. I was spending about a quarter of my time on the road, living in hotels, eating poorly, and jet lagged coming and going. Finally, I had heard (unfounded) rumors of closing of offices; I worried constantly about having my people fired.

My productivity drifted toward zero, until I fled a meeting about scheduling recurring meetings and told a friend that I couldn't go back in the building (I did end up going, though it could have been a legendary way to quit); I hit the bottom and stayed there for a while, unable to send those aforementioned emails.

Everything came out fine. I transferred my teams to good homes and took a couple of weeks off, a friend welcomed me to join his team as an engineer, and after maybe four months of more restorative coding, I was back near full steam.

My situation was bad; hindsight hasn't changed that analysis. But my after-the-fact conclusion is that I mostly had only myself to blame:

- I triaged very poorly, tried to do every single thing available to do, and totally failed to protect my personal life from work; I almost never refreshed myself, and my productivity steadily declined. I'm quite sure I could have done much more by trying to do much less.

- I indulged in constant worry about the possible tragedies of failure. I was right to care about the outcomes for my teams but needed to find some way to accept that risk was part of that situation without constant worry.

One of the lessons may be that I'm not built for high-stakes poker; I hope that's not the truth. I'm sure, however, that I could have done more and better work by prioritizing ruthlessly and setting firm boundaries.

The second, more important lesson, is that you can go lower than you thought possible and come right back; to me, that's comforting. I hope I'm never that burned out again, but if I am, I'll know that it's not the end of my career.

Day to Day at the Office

Professional Skills

Getting Things Done

This chapter aims to give you a leg up on the mechanics of life away from your IDE. We'll cover tools for organizing projects, time management, record-keeping, meetings, and interviewing candidates. None of these skills are complicated in principle, but all are invaluable for getting results on real teams and showing your teammates that you're a mature professional.

Project Management

Project management is organizing technical work to deliver complex projects: planning, tracking, and communication to divide work into coherent pieces, allocate the right resources, do the right things at the right times, remember the loose ends, and unblock engineers (including ourselves).

This section will argue that you need to be a good project manager and offer a primer on how to get there.

© Daniel Heller 2020

D. Heller, *Building a Career in Software*, https://doi.org/10.1007/978-1-4842-6147-7_5

Motivation

At every scale except the tiny bugfix, engineering work demands organization. Project costs must be estimated and weighed against returns; work must divided to map onto engineers; schedules must be communicated to stakeholders; key pieces must be tracked so what ships is complete.

One-person projects (which are uncommon!) require engineers to own every aspect of a project. At the other extreme, 50-person projects may have dedicated project managers, but engineers still need to manage their own work and understand how it interacts with other teams'. In between, engineers need to rise to the task of leading small teams themselves. At every level, engineers must own their own timelines, break their own work into individual tasks/diffs, and cross all their Ts to ship.

Therefore, successful engineers are usually excellent project managers and successful engineering managers doubly so. You should be capable of managing a project as well as a professional project manager, just as the best technical project managers can dig into technology when they have to. And, since we hold ourselves accountable for the success of large projects, we need to be ready to step into project management duties at any time to shepherd a team or area to success. Even now, for the past year, I haven't had a TPM[1] for a ten-person slice of a larger project, so I've been doing it myself.

The Foundation: A List and a Graph

The essence of project management is knowing (a) what needs to be done and (b) how best to deploy people to do it. Therefore, the essential methods common to all project management are

- Keeping a list of all outstanding tasks—a spreadsheet, text file, JIRA board, whatever.

- Understanding the dependency graph of those tasks—a flowchart or a DAG[2] where an edge from A to B says that B can't be done until A is.

These methods establish what needs to be done and how much can be done in parallel; they inform prioritization by showing which project stalls are critical (because they block other work) and which are harmless; they ensure that no known work is forgotten before you release.[3] Armed with those

---

[1]Technical project manager.
[2]Directed Acyclic Graph.
[3]Obviously you may still fail to realize that some work exists, but you won't lose it once you identify it.

constructs, you can estimate timelines, ask for resources, run meetings, and send updates to stakeholders.

The importance of a task-tracking list speaks more or less for itself. I personally am not an enthusiast of the rigid formalism of task-tracking software, but for complex projects where N people may discover work that needs to be tracked and collaboratively solved by the group, it's a must—so if people discover something that needs to be solved, they can fire off a task (for a discussion of to-do lists, see "Productivity and Organization"). A spreadsheet visualization is almost always useful for a large project, too—not necessarily of every single task but certainly of big pieces—so they can be visually consumed on a single, clear screen. For a small project, you may choose to have only a spreadsheet, to-do list, or text file for yourself. Figure 5-1 is an example spreadsheet you might use:

	A	B	C	D
1	Area	Owner	Status	Notes
2	DB Migration	Sarah	In Progress	Double-writing in place, still working on backfill script
3	Network automation	Ying	Not Started	Dealing with production escalation, intend to start next week
4	Routing Logic	Ying	Done	
5	Disaster Recovery	Cody	In Progress	Prototype works, need to refactor and add testing+error handling

Figure 5-1. *Example task list*

The graph may be less obvious. It serves two purposes.

First, it informs prioritization. Engineers always want to start on the wrong piece of a project—on the most fun piece, on the piece they know best (or least), or on just about anything other than what advances the project the most. When you look at a dependency graph, the nodes with the most outbound edges block most other work—you can see which API needs to be defined for three other tasks to start or realize that the missing tooling is blocking five other teams, while the fun performance optimization can easily be deferred and done anytime. The discipline to do that analysis and start with what matters most is enough to make you an above-average project manager.

Second, it lets you schedule, in the senses both of assigning resources (like a CPU scheduler) and predicting timelines. If your graph is basically a list—each task depends on the previous one and nothing else—then no parallelism is possible. You'll do each piece and feed it into the next, and maybe you'll do it all yourself; the time it takes will be the sum of the individual pieces. If there are no edges in the graph except to the "done" box, then each piece is completely independent and you may have infinite parallelism; the total time might be the max of the times of the individual pieces (modulo the complexities of estimation, discussed later in this chapter).

Figure 5-2 is an example based on a real storage migration; the graph shows the major pieces of that project, from bootstrapping the new cluster to shadowing reads (verification with minimal production risk) to production readiness and shutting down the old cluster. A diagram much like this helped me keep track of the individual steps, their dependencies on each other, and the overall flow of the project.

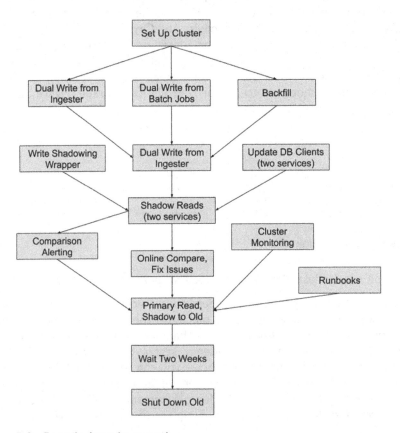

Figure 5-2. Example dependency graph

Keeping Stakeholders Informed

When you manage a consequential project, people want to know how it's going—either because they need to use the results (e.g., they need to use your API) or because your code is their business commitment (e.g., they've promised the feature to a customer or executive).

People care about

1. Timeline
2. What's done
3. What's not done
4. Implications for downstream systems

Managers and project managers usually care more than anything about #1. Technical partners will care about all of the above.

For most projects, we should aim for weekly updates. That cadence establishes a comfortable rhythm where you show a commitment to transparency, and people never wait long enough to start feeling that they're in the dark. For projects under critical pressure, for example, in day-for-day slip against a deadline, briefer daily updates may be appropriate.

We usually update stakeholders one of two ways: email or meetings. Email is the preferred method for large projects, because it can be consumed asynchronously and partially (especially when you have a good tl;dr—see Chapter 13); large status update meetings are strongly discouraged (by me, though they're widely used), because they chiefly consist of tens of highly paid people sitting around, bored, listening only to their own worried thoughts about how they'll word their own update.

For emails, use the project status update email template (Chapter 13). To provide an update in a status meeting, you can use the same template, but strive to be even more brief!

Keeping Close Collaborators Informed

When you're working closely with other engineers, you should communicate far faster and more loosely then with external stakeholders or a big team. I ping close collaborators freely with updates on minor progress and hiccups, ideas I'm having, questions, thanks for their progress, etc. and above all problems that might waste their time—trying to avoid even one second lost to tactical miscommunication and showing them that I value their time, that I want to deliver for them.

I might send chats like the following; these are based on real chats I send every week, with formatting preserved:

- quick fyi—i just landed the build changes, you should be able to adopt the new rule now, please let me know if you have any problems.

- hi anant, sorry i didn't get to your code review earlier. i just added some comments. i'll treat it as my top priority for the rest of the day, so feel free to ping me if you update the diff.

- hey evelyn, I just found a bug in my script. it might not rebuild the coordinator config when you do a dev build. i'm working on a fix right now.

- yo, I just saw that you landed a fix to the reconnect problem we were hitting—that's awesome, thanks so much.

- [to a chat room] hey everybody, if you're seeing failures when turning up a dev cluster, it's probably the bug Jeff is working on. I just landed a fix to the workaround script and updated this channel header with a link to the work-around runbook. sorry for the inconvenience, we'll have a proper fix asap.

These are streaming up-to-the-minute updates, intended to keep people unblocked and productive; these kinds of proactive comms keep collaborators productive and happy, as well as encouraging a broader culture of support.

Schedules and Estimation

Four Laws

Here are my four laws of software schedules. They are intended both to show how schedules and deadlines fit into software engineering businesses and prepare you to estimate effectively:

1. **They're usually artificial, but you still need to care**: Schedules and deadlines sometimes come from real-world constraints, like regulatory deadlines. Much more often, however, they are artificial, born of a desire for predictability in managing a company. Shareholders want to make sound investments with their dollars, which

requires understanding costs and returns; therefore, CEOs must understand returns on engineering investments (e.g., $100,000,000 a year for their engineering department); therefore, CTOs must understand the returns on teams and projects (e.g., $1,000,000 for a substantial project or five engineers for a year); therefore, your manager sure cares about being able to quote a timeline and stick to it. Finally, you should care, because you're accountable to people who look bad if you don't deliver. It can be tempting to feel contempt for artificial deadlines, but disrespecting them won't get you anywhere.

2. **Estimation is the hardest problem in software**: Most software development is fundamentally unpredictable, dominated by the struggle to reveal the true complexity of problems that have not been (in every detail) solved before. Not only is the work itself unpredictable, but your schedule is as well—normal engineering involves frequent interruptions (e.g., a sudden customer problem) that will take up your time and reduce your focus. You will learn quite quickly that you and everyone else are quite bad at estimating how long even a bugfix will take.

3. **Therefore, pad your estimates by 2x**: I've never seen a system for software estimation that was truly accurate; the more complex the system, the less trustworthy. However, padding by 2x seems to be surprisingly effective. Sketch the major pieces of your work, make your best wild guess at how long each will take, add them up, and multiply by 2, and you might come close. As a special case of the principles of doing at least as well as you promise your stakeholders, it's far better to promise late and deliver early than vice versa. Managers and product managers will try desperately to get you to shave time off your estimate; do your darnedest to resist. The 2x multiplier comes partly from inefficiency—we spend less time coding per day than we think—and partly from Simon's Law,[4] which says that productionizing code takes about as long as writing it.

---

[4]Named for one of the best engineers I ever worked with.

4. **Overcommunicate your status**: You're going to slip many schedules in your life (see rule #2). The right time to communicate that you're going to slip is the very first microsecond you're aware of it; if you've chickened out on that first moment, then the second best time is right now. The later the news, the more embarrassing it will be to you and everyone who depends on you, but a prompt, clear notification that a schedule is changing can be a sign of professionalism appreciated by one and all. For example:

> Hi Folks,
>
> Today, we realized that before we can turn on the new session cache, we need a way to shoot down sessions on account deletion. We already have shootdown for password change, but hadn't previously considered the account deletion case. We estimate that this will add a week to the total time to delivery, meaning that our new estimated date for go-live is **March 15th.** Please reach out with any concerns.
>
> Cheers,
>
> Yun

If your manager is going to be angry, that is certainly their professional failing rather than yours, but telling them later is guaranteed to make it worse, not better. If you're on track, you'll still do well to send crisp weekly email summaries of your progress and immediate goals.

Schedules and Estimation: The Basic Algorithm

Now that we've established that careful scheduling is futile and necessary, let's talk about the nuts and bolts of doing it; fair warning that this section won't be rocket science.

Here's my algorithm:

1. Sit down with a pen and paper (it clarifies your thinking better than a laptop).

2. List the major pieces of your work; draw your dependency graph.

3. Estimate the time for each piece.

4. Sum the estimated time for each work item that cannot or will not be done in parallel.

5. Add time for testing; make it much longer than you expect, because you are guaranteed to underestimate.

6. Double the total.

7. Resist requests to reduce that estimate.

This method is simple to the point of obviousness, but I haven't found a better one.

Leading a Project

At any scale, you depend on others' work; as you lead larger projects, you'll depend much more on others' code than on your own. This section will discuss how to shepherd others to a successful delivery of a project.

If you remember only one principle of project leadership, remember that as project lead, your job is to deliver the project, full stop. There's no good excuse for not delivering, and therefore, you can never accept being blocked. You advocate for the resources, you weigh the quality trade-offs, you estimate the timeline, and you persuade and coerce the help you need; when things seem bad, you do the exercise of thinking as if you were your boss,[5] asking yourself which of your assumptions about resources or requirements could be thrown out.

As for the nuts and bolts of leading a project, the foundation is always a firm understanding of a dependency graph; if you don't have that, you don't know whom to ask or what to ask of them. Day to day, you update your map of what's needed, make sure those pieces are spoken for, unblock things that get stuck, mentor people who need it, and adapt your plan and resourcing if circumstances change. Here's my rough algorithm for all of the above:

1. Bootstrap your project understanding by researching and meeting with stakeholders and participants.

2. Draw your actual dependency graph and estimate timeline; write an accompanying concise project plan. Ask participants to estimate and commit to their own timelines.

---

[5] I've found this exercise asking, "what would I do if I had more authority," to be helpful many, many times—because if you know what you would do in your boss's chair, you can go to them with a solution, not a complaint.

3. Communicate this plan and rough timelines (conservatively estimated) to participants.

4. Set up your tracking, as discussed above.

5. Repeat weekly:

    a. **Communicate**: A fair start is a weekly meeting, led by you and ruthlessly kept short, where people give updates and you discuss areas of concern. You may send a weekly status update up the chain or to other stakeholders.

    b. Update your tracking and dependency graph.

    c. Follow-up 1:1 to go deeper on areas of concern or uncertainty.

    d. Review progress against your timelines, and unblock the pieces that get blocked, whether by nagging (see the next section), advising, or doing things yourself. Update stakeholders immediately if timelines change.

    e. Execute on your personal piece of the project.

The Fine Art of Nagging

Follow-up is an essential part of project management—making sure that others really do the things we need them to do, from reviewing changes to building distributed systems out of whole cloth. This section will describe how to nag people to do things you need them to do.

What to Say

As in every other chapter of this book, your primary weapons are honesty and empathy. We start with a strong grasp of the project plan and frankness about what's needed, because we won't get what we need by asking for something else. We encourage, charm, thank, and come through for others so they feel glad to work with us and help us or, at least, less put upon (see Chapter 6). And we apply the minimum emotional force necessary to communicate our needs. The secret ingredient for perfect nagging, though, is acknowledging others' struggles—that they have competing priorities and that your ask may be difficult.

When our partners have committed to a schedule and we have no reason to suspect a problem, our question can be very simple: Are we on track?

Hey Kara, just checking in—are we still on track for rollout in two weeks? Is there anything I can help with?

If the answer is "Yes," we can probably get right back to our own work. Things get much more interesting if you know or suspect that you are not on track; everyone involved is already tense, and we have to find our delicacy. Here's a question I don't like:

Hey Kara, have you fixed that uncaught issue yet? It's blocking the rollout.

Our implication is instantly that Kara should have fixed the bug—that we expect her to, that we're suspicious that she may not have, and that we'll look down on her if she hasn't. Why ask that way when we can ask as a friend?

Hey Kara, have you been able to look at that uncaught bug? I know you were also working on the fallback mechanism, so not sure if you've had a chance, but we do need it for the rollout.

To me, this is all the difference in the world—we're signaling that we care about this bug, reminding Kara that it exists and that she should solve it, and communicating its priority—but we're not implying any judgment. On the contrary, we're acknowledging that she's doing important work and that she may have a good reason for not yet giving us what we need. Here's another empathetic example:

Hey Youssef. I wanted to check in with you about your progress on the secrets migration. How are things going? I know your team's usage is a bit unusually complicated—do you folks have the resources to get this done by the end of the month, or would some help from the secrets side be useful?

Here, we're acknowledging that an ask we've made may be particularly tricky—that a team may have a good reason for being behind schedule. However, at the same time, we're sending the message that the deadline matters and we want to work with them to hit it.

In short, we've nagged well—we've said what we need while encouraging our colleague.

When Gentle Requests Don't Work

Figure 5-3 is my flowchart when gentle requests fail.

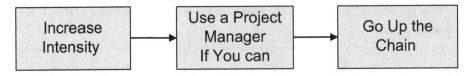

Figure 5-3. Standard escalation path

Increasing the intensity still means talking person to person; it just means expressing urgency.

Hey Vijay, just following up again about the uncaught bug. Sorry to keep bugging you, but this has now become a major problem for the on-call rotation; would you be able to look at it today?

This is the natural evolution of the strategy from the previous section. We prefer it over involving other people, because it's more personal and involves less risk of embarrassment for our colleague.

If that fails, we escalate. Asking a project manager to follow-up is the next incremental escalation; it's milder than going to an engineering manager, because project managers' essential function is to understand outstanding work and ensure that it happens; their follow-up doesn't involve an implication of negligence, unlike reaching out to someone's manager. If a project manager isn't available, we go to our manager or our colleague's (who may be the same). Our question should always emphasize the task, never the negligence of our colleague.

Hey Sandra, I just want to put this task on your radar; it's been lingering for a while, and I think we need to make sure someone follows-up on it, because it's impacting on-call with several alerts per shift.

I would usually do this with a direct outreach, not with an email to both the engineer and their manager. Reaching out to both at once is the last step of escalation, because emailing an engineer and their manager is always accusation of negligence. Sometimes we really need an attitude adjustment from our colleagues, and that's how we can do it. In either case, the admonishment above applies—focus on the task and its impact, not on the negligence.

Advanced Unblocking: Doing It Yourself

I'll mention one advanced technique, not to be used too lightly. When someone fails to follow-up, you can just do their job for them. This might solve your problem, and it might set an inspiring example of vigor and ownership. It can also send a positive message—if your partners really wanted to help but simply couldn't find cycles, and you do it the same way they would, as a partner, you're a friend.

Hi Francisco. Since I know your team is slammed, I thought I might take a shot at this project to unblock the bigger effort. I'll check in with you along the way and make sure your team approves the design and code. What do you think?

On the other hand, if you go rogue and build an alternative in secret, you've shamed them, which you should never do lightly, but sometimes it's necessary.

I once saw a team constantly promise the moon and deliver nothing on a key component for a full year (a debugging tool)—its lack was blocking a critical project. An engineer I knew built a fully functional hacked-up alternative in a single week. It was a scandal; the other team's manager was eventually censured, tears were shed, and it took countless meetings to smooth over the tension between the teams. On the other hand, the project got unblocked. I guess you see the trade-off.

How Often to Follow-up

There's no easy recipe for scheduling your follow-up. All I can say is, err toward less when you can, because it's stressful to be asked for status. For a critical production issue, every 120 seconds is appropriate; for a broken tool that's blocking engineers, maybe once an hour; for a tricky bug blocking a release, once or twice a day; and for an important project that needs to land months in the future, once every week or two.

When I've settled on a wait time, I set a timed reminder in my to-do list app to ensure I won't forget ("two days from today: ask Kara about the schema change"). Following-up reliably, like many feats of quotidian organization, is more impressive than you'd think.

Paying for Information

Estimation is so hard because software projects are filled with unknowns; part of the beauty of our craft is that there are such spectacular ranges of methods and tradeoffs available to us on almost every task. Therefore, early in a project, information is our most precious commodity. We need to swiftly illuminate the map and understand where our challenges will actually lie; therefore, we prioritize tasks that yield information and reduce uncertainty, and we may make quality trade-offs to race past pieces we're confident about. Generally, we ask: What puts this project at risk, and how can we reduce that risk as quickly as possible?

"Prototyping," that is, building fast and at low quality, is a tool for that purpose—when we need information, we buy it by building something optimized for answering our most important questions without agonizing over the tricky error handling, the perfect abstraction, complete observability, etc.

Much is made of the value of always building "throwaway" prototypes, and I think that's too extreme—I've seen people build things to throw away when they could have built right the first time. Prototyping isn't its own reward but a way to pay a favorable price for a lot of information; we should neither fear throwing away code nor resist, when possible, paying a little more for code we can reuse.

Effective Meetings

Meetings can be powerful tools to reach consensus and keep projects on track; they can also be, and usually are, time-wasting nightmares. Good meetings have clear goals agreed on by one and all; stay focused on achieving those goals, and minimize the time to achieve them, and they produce clear plans for action after the fact. Bad meetings do pretty much anything other than that, but especially, they meander without a goal or end without a plan.

Running good meetings is a game changer for making progress on controversial or cross-functional issues. In case that alone doesn't motivate you to read on, I'll note that, like many neglected soft skills among engineers, you're apt to surprise and delight both peers and bosses if you can run a solid meeting; it's well worth your time to study up and find opportunities to practice.

Here are the ingredients of effective meetings:

- **Throughout**: An owner who takes overall responsibility for making a meeting productive

- **Before**: A clear agenda, with context, sent out beforehand

- **During**: Punctuality, minimal distraction, and above all, steady focus on reaching conclusions as quickly as possible

- **After**: Clear meeting notes sent afterward to confirm the decisions of the meeting

Let's explore each in detail.

Throughout: An Owner

Meetings tend toward entropy—all of our efforts are toward turning a naturally chaotic system of different people with different context, goals, and responsibilities, into a productive, organized process. Just like any other task you want done, someone needs to own the fight against meeting entropy—to make sure that the preparation, conversation, and follow-up happen smoothly.

The meeting owner takes on that responsibility. It's seldom a formal role, but you'll find that in productive meetings, someone steps up to take ownership. Most importantly, when you call a meeting to achieve one of your goals, you should personally guarantee the other key ingredients for a successful meeting—send the agenda, shepherd an efficient conversation, and write the meeting notes. Sometimes, one person may call a meeting but (explicitly!) delegate ownership to another attendee.

Before: Agenda

Before any meeting, the owner should write up the meeting's goals and a list of steps to achieve them; the write-up should link to relevant context. That agenda can be included in the meeting invite, sent by email, or both. This up-front communication lets attendees prepare (read, think about the issue), but, perhaps more importantly, it focuses them on the goals—if they know what you need, they can help achieve it. Perhaps most importantly, it requires the meeting owner (you) to think through the goals and method!

Suppose this is a meeting about an infrastructure decision. Here's what an agenda, included in a meeting invitation, might look like:

Calendar Invitation Title: Meeting re. Database Choice for Next Gen Backend

Calendar Invitation Body:

The goal of this meeting is to make a plan for deciding on the database for our next generation backend.

- How to evaluate performance.

- Sketch budget and possible tradeoffs.

- Confirming level of support from Infrastructure team.

- Back of envelope analysis of impact on system design.

- Owners for follow-up in each area.

Manuel will open the meeting with a brief review of scalability issues with the current system and the known requirements for next generation.

Pooja will then give an overview of the infra team's initial investigation and the short list of options to consider.

Finally, we'll have open discussion on the preceding points in that order.

This invite explains the goals of the meeting in some detail. It explicitly calls out owners for providing context in the meeting and links to some detailed background for attendees to prepare themselves.

You may ask: What about long status meetings where everyone gives their report and others have a chance to listen and give feedback? I'm not a fan. However, sometimes the pure information sharing can be valuable to catch problems on complex projects; my advice to you is, in that case, push hard to make everyone move fast and to make everyone else pay attention—try to get the information truly shared and everyone back on task.

During: Punctuality

Lateness wastes others' time and sets a tone of poor focus. Set a tone of businesslike precision, with the expectation that you'll start on time and get done early, and everyone will improve their focus and efficiency. You don't need to wait for everyone to arrive to start; you have quorum when all key decision-makers and technical experts have arrived.

During: Start with Agenda Review

Once you reach quorum, the meeting owner should start by reviewing the agenda. Some attendees will have failed to read it; others will have forgotten; everyone will benefit from a brief, clear refresher to nudge them in the right direction.

Thanks for coming, everyone! As you know, we've decided to move off of SimpleDB for our next gen backend, and we need to decide how our teams will work together to make the choice.

Our goals in this meeting are to confirm a plan for choosing a database, especially identifying an owner and PoCs for driving the decision, but also running through key concerns for performance testing, budget trade-offs, and ownership/support.

Manuel will start by reviewing the current system's problems and requirements we know about, and then Pooja will discuss the options the DB team has come up with in their initial investigation. After that we'll talk about performance, budget, support, and next steps/owners.

Let's get started—Manuel?

Now you're ready to get down to business.

During: Focus on Reaching Conclusions

Every meeting should achieve actionable conclusions, reviewed succinctly at the end of the meeting—otherwise, how is anyone better off? If a meeting doesn't seem to be moving toward actionable conclusions, you should try to push it there—notably, any discussion that isn't helping should be swiftly deferred (or just dropped); your colleagues are well-paid professionals, and every minute of their time is money spent. You'll find that when you successfully refocus a meeting, your peers will be surprisingly impressed and appreciative; for a long time, this was my only skill, and I seemed to get by better than you'd think. You can say things like:

What would help us reach a conclusion here?

Could we table this for now and focus on <the main question>?

This is definitely an important question, but since we're short on time, maybe we should move on to the next topic and circle back later?

I'm not sure if we can decide this right here—<person>, maybe you could analyze this offline and email us your assessment?

Do we have the right people to figure this out? Should we pause this conversation until we can get input from <an expert>?

During: Review Action Items

If anything needs to happen based on the discussions in a meeting, the meeting should end with a review of clear action items with clear owners. If something needs to be done and doesn't have an owner, it will not get done.

Okay, so our action items are: **Erika** to send guidance to the team and **Donald** to start the rollout tomorrow morning. I'll send the meeting notes.

After: Meeting Notes

When a good meeting is over, someone (agreed on at the meeting, by default the meeting owner) should usually send crisp meeting notes reviewing the purpose of the meeting, who attended, what was discussed, what was concluded/agreed on, and what the action items are (with owners). Within one team, or at a small company, formal notes may not be necessary, but when multiple teams are involved, a write-up minimizes the risk of conflicting memories of what you agreed on. Otherwise, you can hit some nasty conflict down the line, like two people each think the other is going to write a certain piece of code. Here's an example of my typical meeting notes:

Email Subject: Meeting Notes for Database Migration Sync 2020-02-29

Email Body:

Subject: How to decide on database system for next-generation backend

Attendees: Angie, Ferras, Chris, Syrie, Song, DeMarcus, Manuel, Pooja

Notes:

- According to Jing, feedback from Infra team is that BuggyDB is fully supported, but AgamemnonDB support is still in experimentation phase.

- Concerns about replication reliability with BuggyDB are not sufficiently severe to warrant ruling it out, we'll move forward with performance experiments.

- Action Items:

- **Syrie** will confirm infrastructure budget for this migration w/Donald .

- **Song & Chris** will take point on the performance investigation (report within a week)

- **Angie** will follow up with Infra team about timelines for full AgamemnonDB support.

This is a comprehensive but formal structure. If that formality seems out of place on your team (ask a colleague!) but you still want to record your conclusions, you can try something simpler:

Email Subject: Meeting Notes for Database Migration Sync 2020-02-29

Email Body:

Hi all,

Just recording our conclusions from this meeting: we decided that Song and Chris will go ahead with the performance investigation of BuggyDB, Syrie will check on the budget for the migration, and Angie will check on the AgamemnonDB support. Thanks everyone!

Cheers,

DH

A Note on Meeting Etiquette

Formality scales with the size of a meeting and the stature of the attendees; that means that we're on our best behavior with large groups, customers, senior colleagues, and above all senior leadership (e.g., your boss's boss). You can call that an old-fashioned perspective if you like, but lots of people who make career-altering decisions have old-fashioned manners, and it's easier to show respect than correct a bad impression. That means no to

- Slouching or leaning back our chairs
- Reading our phones or laptops unless strictly necessary
- Interrupting
- Edgy jokes
- Bad-mouthing others
- Complaining

It means yes to

- Respectfully but proactively introducing ourselves
- Paying attention
- Waiting our turn to speak
- Not dominating the conversation
- Giving everyone a chance to say their piece; making space for the shy or quiet and soliciting their opinions (especially if you're the meeting chair!)

I'll also offer a puritanical perspective on one key part of meetings: people shouldn't open their laptops if it can be avoided. If a meeting is so poorly run that people need to kill time, it should be improved or canceled; if your colleague is going to the trouble of speaking for your benefit, you should pay them the respect of your full attention.

Productivity and Organization

Time Management and To-Do Lists

When I started out in software (and before that, in college, high school, middle school, and elementary school), I constantly forgot things I needed to do. I've solved this problem with the diligent use of a to-do list app, and it's wildly increased productivity and reliability; you should do the same.

Here's the number one technique that's made the biggest difference: my to-do app is synced between my phone and Mac, and every single time something comes up for me to do, I instantly drop it into the app. That magic trick wasn't available when I started my career, but it means the world to me, because I've entirely stopped worrying that I'm forgetting something important at any given time. I use the app Things, but others use Evernote, Omniplan, etc., etc., etc.; the only features you need are

- Data must be shared between phone and desktop, so you can create to dos wherever you are (e.g., immediately after a hallway conversation).

- Creating a simple to do should be frictionless, so you do it.

If you adopt only this practice, it'll be quite beneficial, but I got even more benefit when I read a book I highly recommend, David Allen's *Getting Things Done*.

GTD has many compelling (if unscientific) things to say about the psychology of focus and stress, but I'll summarize it for you briefly here: if you build an organizational system you trust that allows you to quickly see what the best thing to do is at any given time, you free your mind from constant decision-making and worrying about what you're forgetting—this should enable you to pick one thing at a time and apply yourself with laser focus. The key innovations on top of diligent list making are:

- Keeping contextual lists (e.g., work and home)

- Regularly reviewing and prioritizing your list of tasks, making sure that you can quickly find the most urgent ones in any given context when it's time to work; the regular grooming improves your confidence that you're doing the right thing at any given time and therefore reduces your stress.

Read the book.

Effective Calendaring

Using a digital calendar is a pretty simple business: you invite other people; you don't schedule meetings early in the morning or when your counterparties are already booked. I'm going to offer just a couple of tips that will make you seem like a real pro to (grateful) busy people.

- Always include a video conference link. People work from home all the time and get held up here or there; make it easy on them.

- Give your attendees edit permissions on the invite (if your system supports it), and tell them that: "You have edit rights on this invite, please feel free to move it to a more convenient time." Busy people's calendars will shift, and you want to make it easy for them to reschedule.

- Include a crisp agenda in your meeting invite; mention each topic you plan to cover and what the *goals* of the meeting should be (it's not just a chitchat session; it has a goal).

Subject: Timeline for Project Hufflepuff

- Schedule risks from DB migration

- Tax compliance implications

Goal: Confirm a deadline that can be communicated outside the org.

- Defragment other people's time; if they have a packed calendar, try to find a slot adjacent to their other meetings, and especially try to avoid creating small gaps between meetings. Most people are most effective in contiguous blocks of focused time, and you should help them create that space.

- When scheduling by email, always offer a menu of acceptable times (with explicit time zones if you're in different ones!):

Meeting next week sounds great. Would one of the following slots work?

Monday 2/1: 11 AM PT or 2 PM PT

Wednesday 2/3: 1:30 PM PT

Caching Knowledge

Every day, you're going to figure out useful things by reading documentation, asking people questions, and painstaking trial and error. The following day, you'll have to do the same things, and for all but a few rare geniuses, you're guaranteed to have forgotten the ten flags to curl that finally made your test work; therefore, you'll again need to either waste your own time or someone else's. Your goal should be to have every learning you extract improve your future efficiency, and your solution is to keep two documents:

- An infinitely scrolling Google Doc, your cheat sheet, with a little section for each neat trick you figure out. This document should record things you might not otherwise know how to do—it is a durable repository of knowledge.

- A text file on your computer, your command cache, with commands you've been using particularly recently. These may or may not be hard to figure out, but they would take time to reconstruct; just copy–paste! A text file is less durable than a Google Doc, but it's much faster for frequent use.

There may be overlap between these two documents; the command cache is ultimately just for convenience and speed, but the cheat sheet is for saving the day when your memory doesn't come through for you.

Scripting Everything

This advice is quoted just about everywhere, so I'll be brief: if you type a command more than five times, you should script it, ideally down to five characters or less (e.g. gco for git checkout), either as a shell script or an alias. You'll improve your shell scripting and save yourself endless time and wrist pain. I strongly recommend keeping your Git repository of personal shell scripts (see "Living in the Cloud") in your path; if you go two weeks without adding a new script, you're probably not automating enough.

To give you a sense of how completely your life should be mediated through automation, below are my favorite git aliases; even though the full commands are short, I consider it completely worthwhile to save single-digit keystrokes for a common operation, and you'd be surprised how many engineers have the exact same aliases.

Command/Alias	Definition
gb	git branch
gd	git diff
gdc	git diff --cached
gg	git grep
gs	git status

Living in the Cloud

All your dotfiles and scripts should be in a private Git repository (I use GitHub); all your documents should be safely striped to a hundred servers (I use Google Docs); getting a new laptop set up to be productive shouldn't cost you more than a half hour, and you should never even think about "restoring from backup"—the cloud should be the truth.

Just Do Something

Perhaps the easiest way to separate effective and ineffective engineers is into those who Do Something when they encounter a problem and those who... do anything other than Something, like talking about how things could be better, waiting for someone else to solve it, or ignoring it. This virtue is sometimes called a bias to action. Managers and colleagues love people who do things rather than complaining or waiting for other people (their parents? their nanny?) to do them.

This problem arises around half the time from a misunderstanding of one's role—staying blocked because the blocker "isn't my job," when in fact, your job is to get results even when you hit a roadblock.

In the other half, it comes from a lack of confidence—a paralysis induced by the discomfort and fear of not knowing exactly what to do. It's true that responding to an unexpected challenge with vigor requires confidence in one's ability to improvise. It's also true that in some delicate situations, where some of the things you can do might have serious consequences, it's best to ask for help or spend time thinking carefully—but that's still much better than doing literally nothing, and colleagues will be much happier to help you if you show that you've tried your best (and ask your question <u>clearly - see Chapter 14</u>).

Here are a few examples where I regularly see people do absolutely nothing when they could do something.

Issue	Why I Can't Do Something	Yes You Can! Try This
We're blocked waiting for another team's bugfix	They haven't commented on the bug	Email the engineer. Email their manager. Walk over to their area. Chat someone. Call them on the phone. Ask your manager or a more senior person to escalate
Requests are failing	I don't know what dashboard to look at	Search for the service name on the metrics home page. Guess the name. Look at a global dashboard. Call someone and ask. @here in a chat room and ask. Page someone else
We can't land changes because the build is broken	I don't know how the build works	Figure it out! Ask someone. Go to the Jenkins page and find the logs. Use git bisect, which lets you find the culprit even without semantic understanding
My colleague blocked my diff with code review comments I disagree with	He's too obstinate, I can't make progress	Meet face to face with the colleague, and try to understand the feedback better. Get a second opinion from a colleague you trust, and ask if they have an idea for how to handle it tactfully. Ask your manager for advice or to intervene. Just go around them (if circumstances allow it)

Keep a Worklog

I keep a log of every single thing I do at work—every bug I fix, every proposal I write, every outage I work on, every presentation I give, and every person I mentor and what I mentor them about. I keep that list because sooner or later, I always have to tell the story of what I've been doing—for an annual self-review, a promotion case, or just a status report—and it's almost impossible to do without some kind of written record. I use my to-do list method from <u>Time Management and To-Do Lists</u> to maintain the list; when I do something useful, I write a super fast to-do:

> worklog: incident commander for configuration service
> outage 10/14

Then I asynchronously process those to dos and put them into my doc, which is divided into a section for each quarter of the year (a common cadence of reporting). Start today.

Hiring Engineers: Interviewing from the Other Side of the Table

A Controversial Assertion

No one knows a reliable way to measure the difference between a good engineer and a bad one; therefore, no one knows how to interview engineers, and we are obliged to rely on intuition, with all its flaws. Anyone who tells you that they do know how, and many people will, is arrogant; the best you can hope for is a relatively persuasive intuition.

A good interview process would select for engineers that help the company succeed; the rigorous design of that process would require first telling the difference between high-performing engineers and low performers, then identifying qualities that predict good performance. For example, if we asked the same 5 questions of 1,000 hires, and knew which performed well and which poorly, we could try to figure out which questions gave the strongest indication of future success.

In reality, we don't even know who is truly a high performer and who a low performer; in this domain as well, we rely fully on our intuition—managers basically just use their judgment. And even with the data we do have (i.e., internal performance reviews, flawed though they are), I personally haven't encountered attempts to assess the predictive power of interviewing methodologies.

Therefore, you can rest easy that no one really knows how to select engineers. Still, we have to decide with the information we have (usually four to five one-hour interviews) and complaining that it can't be done rigorously isn't a solution, howsoever great the pleasure it gives me. What should we do?

Interview Focus Areas

If we can't rely on science, we must rely on the best of our reasoning and intuition; in this section, I'll talk about the qualities I look for, how I look for them, and how I put it all together into a decision.

I think many blends of skills can be successful in software, and when we're hiring, we should keep an open mind to that variety of possibilities—a good team has room (indeed, the need) for collective excellence in every domain but doesn't need every individual to shine in every domain. If you'll forgive my reciting what's now a cliché, we should resist with all our energy the desire to hire people who strongly resemble ourselves lest we both commit illegal, immoral discrimination and deny our teams the benefit of a variety of perspectives. You would do quite well to review the forms of <u>illegal discrimination in hiring</u> (which vary by US state and country).

This lesson was brought home for me by working with an awesome engineer I would never at that time have hired. He was for all intents and purposes impossible to communicate with, and I personally prize good communication in colleagues; he frustrated me literally every time I crossed paths with him. However, he was a consummate *doer*. He didn't complain, he didn't brag, he just went and found really tricky stuff that needed doing and did it, especially around a database system that was causing us a lot of problems; our team would have been in big trouble without him. It was humbling for me to see that he was what our team needed even though he wasn't what *I* looked for (and in fact, even though I didn't love working with him).

Despite these arguments for doubting ourselves, we need to do our best. Here are the unoriginal dimensions on which I try to evaluate potential engineering hires. I'll summarize briefly, then discuss each at some greater length. I don't define a strong priority order on areas in general, though I weight architecture and domain knowledge less for engineers early in their careers.

- Coding (we write code)
- Architecture (we design systems)
- Communication (we almost always work with others)
- Domain knowledge (knowing stuff helps you do stuff)
- Organized thinking (button mashing doesn't solve hard problems)
- Attitude (dedication and respect for others pull the package together)

Coding

Why: it's ultimately what we do, and engineers should show fluency in at least one programming language to give us confidence that they will be comfortable producing code.

How: A coding problem, ideally in a shared editor like CodePair (so you can see how they really code!). I personally do think that coding problems should, to the greatest extent possible, not be centered on one crucial little trick—there should be a smooth curve of potential outcomes, not just total success or total failure—but you can bet I don't have science to back me up. However, I do have the intuition that coding under pressure is hard and finding a little trick doesn't come up that often in my job.

I do prefer a coding question to include some basic data structure concepts, though it shouldn't simply be a test of CS102 knowledge; while data structures expertise may be a shibboleth of sorts, it does seem to correlate with the accumulation of other useful knowledge in my personal experience.

I try to pay attention so I can observe the candidate's process but, at the same time, make it explicitly clear that if they want to take time to think without interacting with me, that's fine—I want to reduce the extreme "performance art" dimension of the live coding interview.

What to Look For

- Comfort with their programming language of choice, showing that they really code professionally and have developed ease with their tools.

- A methodical approach, as opposed to chaotic/guess and check; developing a mental model of the code that they can describe and walk you through. As an interviewer, I hope that they will bring a similarly scientific approach to their work.

- Comfort with basic data structures; this is, to a degree, more of a signal between engineers that it is a direct evaluation of skills needed for success, but data structures do come up.

Example Questions

- Write a program that can check whether a Sudoku solution is correct.

- Write a program to find a solution to the N-queens problem.

Architecture

Why: Engineers have to design systems, which requires reasoning about technical trade-offs and seeing a picture bigger than an individual line of code.

How: Three key approaches

- Discussions of existing technologies, their properties, and trade-offs between them.

- Design problems requiring a candidate to design a real system (typically on a whiteboard).

- Exploring past projects, examining design trade-offs and alternatives.

What to Look For

- Ability to maintain a reasonable level of abstraction, that is, avoiding getting sidetracked by small details and instead composing an overall picture of the system they are designing. Excessive focus on details is generally an obstacle to reasoning about system design.

- Ability to articulate key design concerns and discuss trade-offs in their approach; a candidate should clarify what exactly the requirements of a system are and demonstrate a sound reasoning process that would generalize to a variety of problems. That means that they don't just make good choices but that they're able to articulate why they made them for this specific problem and why alternative approaches were rejected.

- Staying on topic and solving the problem you're asking about, not some other problem they want to solve.

- Some knowledge of the key domain technologies (depending on their level of experience and the specificity of the role); particularly, more experienced candidates should usually show that they have made an investment in learning in their chosen domain, such that if asked to design a system, they could reason intelligently about the components available to choose from. I personally believe that this knowledge is quite undervalued in most hiring processes—a lot of work requires people to know things. Obviously, there may be exceptions to this criteria—junior candidates, or those transferring across domains, may show promise that justifies forgoing deep domain expertise.

Example Questions

- Design Twitter.

- Design an iOS app for online chess.

- Tell me about a tough design problem you've worked on in the past. [Then, for important elements of the design] What were the alternatives, and why did you choose this approach?

Communication

Why: Most substantial engineering work requires collaboration.

How: I don't suggest a dedicated interview for this area. Instead, this dimension should be evaluated in all interviews.

What to look for: You're looking for two things: good listening and clear self-expression. Good listening means that the candidate is able to gather the essence of a problem from you, asking good clarifying questions as needed. Clear self-expression means that they can convey their own ideas back to you. There are no simple rules for evaluating this, but I suggest paying particular attention to whether a candidate has understood what exactly you've asked them and whether, when asked clarifying questions, they can answer on topic, completely, and succinctly.

Domain Knowledge

Why: In my opinion, performance on puzzly interview coding questions is overrated, and deep domain knowledge is wildly underrated. I am almost wholly unsympathetic to the oft-quoted, "I'd rather have someone who can learn than someone who has just memorized stuff"—personal experience is that when things get tricky, the people who deeply understand the systems involved, be they databases, languages, cloud systems, or whatever, will save your bacon, and people who "know how to learn," admirable though they may be, will still be tying their shoes when the knowledgeable people cross the finish line. Try to hire engineers who know stuff!

How: An architecture interview can be a good place to dive in on domain knowledge; ask probing follow-up questions and see how deep a candidate can go on a given technology. I also once had an interview with a firm that just asked me 50 or so pure knowledge questions, one after another—I thought it was a radical and interesting approach given the norms of that time, and it might serve you well too.

What to look for: Knowing stuff, being able to contextualize and apply it in a fluid way as you ask questions (ref. organized thinking, communication).

Example Questions

- Can you tell me what people mean when they talk about trade-offs between consistency and availability in database systems?

- Can you tell me what happens when I type a domain name into a browser address bar and press "Enter"?

Organized Thinking

Why: Substantial engineering problems require navigating between high and low levels of abstraction (design and implementation), prioritizing between varied tasks, and identifying dependencies between tasks. You want a signal that your candidate will approach complex, varied sets of tasks deliberately, without becoming paralyzed by the variety of choices at any given moment.

How: This area should be emphasized in the architecture interview, which requires the most navigation of different levels of abstraction. However, like communication, it can be observed in every interview.

What to look for: You should look for a smooth flow from understanding requirements to identifying key design problems to choosing components. You should consider it a red flag if a candidate jumps rapidly between different levels of abstraction without trying to deduce stage N from stage N-1.

Attitude

Why: Two reasons. First, I haven't yet met a level of brilliance that I consider to make up for disrespect—my experience is that one jerk can poison a whole team. Second, even the most perfectly prepared genius needs passion, dedication, and humility to adapt to changing circumstances, find common ground with others, and take responsibility.

How: We mostly take aim at attitude with questions about experience, interests, and goals, but it can surface through any question. An experience or "manager" interview is the obvious time to explore these areas, but I'll often sprinkle a question or two at the beginning of a technical interview just to round out the picture.

What to look for: I look for two things: passion (enthusiasm for technology and/or problem-solving) and a collaborative attitude (respect for others and willingness to compromise).

Passion doesn't mean effusion—quiet people can do great work and never singing songs about it. However, I expect engineers to articulate some interest in technology or in real-world problems—problems they'd like to tackle, skills they'd like to learn, technologies they think are cool.

It's easier to find red flags when it comes to interpersonal attitude than it is to prove excellence. Candidates should know better than to bad-mouth past colleagues or show contempt for your questions.

Example Questions

- What are you looking for in the next few years of your career?

- What technologies are you interested in working with?

- Tell me about a time you had to deal with conflict on a project.

- Tell me about a coworker you've admired in the past and what you learned from them.

The Nuts and Bolts of Interviewing

This section will describe how I personally plan and execute an interview; it's not the only way, but it's a fine way to start.

First, before the interview, I review a candidate's resume, decide what questions I'll ask, and plan the schedule down to the minute. Why such careful planning? This is because the most common failure mode for interviewers is to fall down a rabbit hole on a minor point and end up with no signal, and that is 100% on the interviewer when it happens; I plan my time and watch the clock.

I start every interview by smiling; introducing myself by name, team, and specialty; then telling the candidate what we'll cover in the interview. In a competitive hiring environment and as a matter of principle, the candidate should feel at all times that they're welcome, that your energy is positive, and that their experience is well-organized; a smile and an overview are a good start. You'll cultivate your own manner, but I try to be professional, calm, and breezy—commiserating and laughing when I can, trying to lower the intensity and praise progress. Some interviewers favor a cold, withdrawn style, thinking that it forces the candidates to "step up" more—I disagree, as comfort with jerks isn't an important criterion for me in a candidate.

I almost always follow with a gentle warm-up question about a simple technical problem. This gives people a chance to loosen up for the tougher questions and also lets me see how they communicate material they know quite well. For example, I might ask, "tell me about what a hash table is and what its properties are."

If I have an hour, I might also ask a question about their experience; either way, I'll allocate most of the interview for the main question, either a coding or design problem. I suggest you source some of these from colleagues or from the many Internet problem banks.

Finally, I'll allocate five minutes for them to ask questions, which is also a chance for me to chat with them, encourage them to relax, and sell them on why my company is a great place to work; even if they failed my interview, they may ace every other one, and I want to do my part to close them.

Given these pieces, my schedule might look like this:

> 45-minute interview
>
> 2 minutes: Introduction
>
> 3 minutes: Interests question
>
> 5 minutes: Basic data structures question
>
> 30 minutes: Coding problem
>
> 5 minutes: Q&A

During the interview, I proactively manage the clock; you should feel free to redirect the candidate if they get stuck or just to say, "Great! That's an interesting discussion, but we need to move on to the next question to stay on schedule." My schedule bakes in some time for the candidate to struggle, and when they do, I let them (a bit); you want to see how they react when really challenged. However, I don't let a candidate make zero progress for more than a few minutes; at that point they're probably really stuck, and there's no more to be gained from withholding a nudge.

Finally, throughout the interview, I take detailed notes; I use my own shorthand to capture what I say, what they say, and general observations (something like italics for what I say, quotes for what they say, brackets for observations). This is quite important, because you will forget most details within the first hour after the interview. Some people prefer paper to a laptop for this purpose, because a laptop can really feel "between" the interviewer and the candidate.

Decisions

You've heard my skepticism about any supposed objectivity of hiring decisions. Therefore, the only way to make decisions is intuition, and the main way to calibrate is experience. So, your first few decisions are going to be very rocky, and that's okay. Ask your questions to a bunch of candidates, and you'll get a sense for where people struggle and what average performance looks like; see how your respected colleagues evaluate candidates you've interviewed, and try to refine your process. I've had a great experience with mock interviews—interviewing a great colleague as if they were a candidate. A great teammate should crush the interview—if they do, you know your question at least isn't unreasonably hard, and they may have good feedback on what is and isn't clear.

Software Methodologies and the Generality of Good Engineering

All teams have systems for allocating their resources and planning their execution; those methodologies, which fill countless books, can range from the highly formalized (heard of a Certified Scrum Master?) to the totally improvised. This section will prepare you for some of the common methods you may encounter in the wild.

First, the big picture. In my (possibly controversial) opinion, engineering fundamentals are universal across methodologies. Your priority is always to excel at project management, collaboration, and writing working software, and you can do those things well in any framework much the same way: project management is always about understanding dependencies, staying organized, and conservative estimation; collaboration is always about crisp communication, empathy, and efficient use of your colleagues' time; software that works is software that works. So, don't overthink it!

Still, it's worthwhile to understand your team's system, and we can extract useful insight from the formal methods; we'll discuss a few common elements. Note that if your team uses any formal method, you should study it on your own to see where they're coming from.

Yearly, half-yearly, or quarterly planning are extremely common features of industry life. Companies set a regular cadence where engineering teams and stakeholders—product managers, businesspeople, designers, etc., etc.—meet and/or fight each other to the death to set goals. You should remember two things about these processes. First, the pressure will always be to commit to more, never less; try to gently hold your ground when you believe goals are too ambitious. My refrain is usually along the lines of, "I can only be frank about what I think is realistic." Second, you and your manager will be held accountable for your team's goals. That means that once your team has committed, you should care rather a lot about delivering.

Day to day, it's quite common to see teams do ad hoc planning, that is, distributing work to individuals' queues as it comes in or distributing individuals to work as they finish tasks. This can co-occur with fixed planning cycles, which may decide only high-level goals. Some people find ad hoc planning frustrating and chaotic; I happen to feel that improvisation can be fun and powerful when a team is well-aligned. Hold on tight, and accept that you don't always need to know what you'll do a month in advance! Ad hoc processes demand one specific reminder: when you finish something, you absolutely must go find something else to do, asking your boss if necessary. We don't sit still just because no one is pushing us!

Agile Software Development

Agility is an organization's capacity to adapt to changing circumstances: swift execution, lightweight planning processes, and openness to course corrections. "Agile Software Development," or "Agile," is a class of formal development processes intended to encourage that quality.

Agile principles argue for short development cycles that integrate requirements gathering, design, and development, constantly shipping small increments of working software, bringing together stakeholders and developers to review and assess, and replanning as circumstances change. You can reference the Manifesto for Agile Software Development for a sense of the genesis of this movement, but Wikipedia, or a book like *Essential Scrum*, will offer much more detail.

My experience agrees with these principles: I've seldom seen complexity foreseen in detail, and a short-duration, iterative, open process can contribute to (but don't guarantee) a real ability to swivel toward newly discovered problems and opportunities. Scrum and Kanban are probably the best-known attempts to systematize these concepts. Scrum, the more common, is described below, but it's a good investment to learn something about Kanban's powerful visualizations on your own.

Scrum

Scrum organizes the software development process into a rhythm of self-contained "sprints," typically periods of 1–4 weeks, and codifies specific roles and meetings to structure those sprints. Its essential principle is collaboration, with all team members contributing to planning, implementation, and team introspection and daily helping each other overcome blockers. I find that many teams borrow at least some Scrum methods, especially 2-week sprints as a planning cadence.

The sprint is structured as

- First, a Sprint Planning Meeting where the team works together to set tractable goals for the sprint.

- For the duration of the sprint, a short daily "scrum" or "stand-up," where team members discuss their progress, help each other resolve "blockers" (problems impeding their progress) and cross-pollinate useful information.

- At the end of the sprint, a Sprint Review and a Retrospective for reviewing (and celebrating) progress, demoing results, and identifying opportunities to improve.

Asynchronously, the team regularly reviews and prioritizes ("grooms") a "backlog" of future work. You'll find that teams vary in their adherence to the orthodoxy; sometimes "Scrum" means a radical commitment to iteration and collaboration, and sometimes it just means having a daily meeting.

My experience is that formal scrum-like processes, where a team insists on sprint-length deliverables, can work beautifully for simpler, cohesive projects, where complexity is foreseeable, work easily decomposes into value-adding pieces, and team members share a backlog. I've seen them turn quite awkward and meeting-heavy on the deepest projects, where engineers regularly uncover unpredictable complexity and daily facetime may not add value.

I'd add a few specific tips on top of the general purpose advice above. First, Scrum demands hyperefficiency in meetings, because you meet every day—prepare concise, informative updates in advance. Second, try to make the most of Scrum's daily facetime with teammates: listen, make the most of what teammates share, and try to unblock them. Third, a tight planning cycle can be relatively intolerant of detours (i.e., in some cases less agile); you may need extra diligence about avoiding even value-adding detours.

Working with Humans

This chapter will discuss the social side of professionalism: how to nurture the mutual respect and enjoyment that make professional relationships efficient and fun and how to avoid common engineer misbehaviors that can drive people up the wall. We'll start with advice that applies to more or less all workplace interactions, then move on to more specific challenges—feedback, bosses, and system owners.

General Social Skills

Manners

In my opinion, "having good manners" means putting others at ease—anticipating what causes others stress and taking it out of your interactions, so they can feel secure and peaceful. As noted in many other sections, good manners make a strong impression; I've found that people often remember and appreciate a single act of grace and kindness for years. We'll discuss a few cases where people might feel stress, but you can put them at ease. I'll leave it as an exercise for you to find others in your day-to-day life.

D. Heller, *Building a Career in Software*, https://doi.org/10.1007/978-1-4842-6147-7_6

- Accept apologies eagerly: not "np" but "no worries! Things worked out fine." Let them know you're really fine so they can stop worrying.

- When you go out for lunch, drinks, or anything else that costs money, pay people back absolutely without fail; make sure no one ever feels awkward about whether they'll get their money.

- When you meet any colleague, shake their hand (if that's customary in your area), smile, and introduce yourself; show that you're glad to work with them. Take special care with people junior to you; they're naturally likely to be insecure about their position, and they'll be glad to know you see them as an equal.

- When you lapse in your politeness—by saying something curt, by accidentally wasting someone's time, by cutting someone off, whatever the case may be—apologize thoroughly and earnestly. Help people recover from the discomfort of your rudeness, and show your respect.

- When others reach out to you, respond as promptly as humanly possible, and apologize when you don't; show that you value their time and consider it a commitment to help them.

- Don't interrupt in meetings or conversation. Have you ever felt a breathless, almost painful desire to say the thought that's jumped into your head, even though other people are talking and saying reasonable things? Well, so have I, every single day, but interrupting shows disrespect and makes you seem oblivious. Outwit the impulse.

- Thank people thoroughly every single time they help you—show that you don't take their help for granted.

Giving Credit

One of the most important ways to build trust and mutual appreciation with your colleagues is to scrupulously give them credit when they do good work; one of the easiest ways to enrage someone is to either claim credit for their work or allow others to mistakenly attribute it to you.

Therefore, when someone does something that helps you, or even just that you admire, you should go out of your way (even way out of your way) to acknowledge that good work to them, their manager, and your mutual peers.

The first argument for this practice is aesthetic: one of the greatest satisfactions in professional life is to collaborate with talented, well-intentioned people, get good results together, and share a mutual appreciation; you can gratify your colleagues and yourself by acknowledging their good work.

The second argument is practical, not to say cynical: you want your colleagues to learn the lesson that collaborating with you is beneficial and pleasant so that they're eager to help you again. Note that this doesn't extend to flattery— you're an engineer, not a politician, and deceit is likely to be transparent and will backfire. You should genuinely appreciate good work and share that appreciation from the heart.

When someone does you a good turn, try one of the following:

- **Thank them directly by email or chat**: "Thanks a lot for your help! This saved me a lot of time!"

- **Email feedback to them and their manager**: "Cheng went deep on this problem with me and ended up finding a bug that's been causing crashes for weeks— thanks so much!" I'm quite liberal in sending managers feedback; it's useful for them for writing performance reviews and can give the engineer a real bump.

- **Mention their help in a broader email**: "Special thanks to Guru, whose help on the storage side was essential to hitting this deadline."

- **If a team goes above and beyond for you and your team, get them treats to say "thanks"**: Cupcakes, donuts, or cookies will let them know you really appreciated their work. Your manager may let you expense this.

- **For truly exceptional work, get creative**: I have sometimes bought trophies and given them out.

A Word About Charm and Positivity

I believe in charm among nerds. I use the term "charm" to mean making people feel good and finding common ground with them—building the connection that makes it a pleasure to work together. You should cultivate charm, first, because connecting with your colleagues makes work fun and gratifying and second because strong relationships make projects move more smoothly. This section will offer a few suggestions for doing so.

The fulfillment of connecting with people you work with should speak for itself—when I haven't invested in it, I've always in the long run wished I had.

The professional benefit needs an explanation—and a defense from charges of cynicism.

In a healthy organization, people help all their colleagues; in many teams, not so much. But in every organization, you can get better results by building strong connections with your colleagues and making them feel good about themselves and their team. When people are stressed and busy, they'll go that extra inch to help someone they feel close to; when something is hard and controversial, people will listen more eagerly and more carefully to a friend. So, even if you're one of many engineers who find solitude or shyness natural, as I do, you should go out of your way to make people feel good and find common ground with them—as some would say, to be charming.

How to Win Friends and Influence People is long and dated, but distilled to one sentence, it has the best advice I know for connecting with people: take a genuine interest in others, and give them the benefit of the doubt. When you work with someone, find a chance to engage with them. Ask them how they are. Ask them what they did last weekend. Show them the respect of asking for feedback on a piece of your work. Ask them how their work is going, what they thought of the company meeting, and if they saw the same movie you saw last week. Then, ask follow-up questions; it may not be the entire art of conversation, but by golly it's a start.

If, however, you can remember a few more things, below are a handful of tips I've often thought engineers particularly should remember. Cutting across all of them is one key point: they all depend on honesty, and people will see right through it if you attempt them in bad faith.

- **Finding fault is not a sport**: Engineers often come off like precocious children desperate to prove that they're smarter than a teacher—we love to prove people wrong. And indeed, sometimes people are wrong, sometimes proving that you're right is fun, and sometimes people do need to be corrected. But, the hobby of proving people wrong has two big problems: it's incredibly annoying, and it often doesn't benefit the victim. All in, annoying colleagues for no benefit is a quick way to convince people to avoid you. Sometimes, when people are wrong, you can just let it slide and say nothing; when you have to disagree, you can do it while giving others the benefit of the doubt, as in How to Deliver Criticism. Generally, you'll do better to comment on where you agree with others than where you disagree. Note, though, that this doesn't extend to cases where people really need feedback, and I don't mean to suggest that you should ever misrepresent how you feel—my advice is just to pick your battles, not to always smile and nod.

- **Bring other people up**: Your colleagues are very likely admirable people beset by insecurities and worries, just like you (or at any rate like me). Expressing honest gratitude and admiration—finding qualities and actions you genuinely admire and commenting on them when the situation calls for it—giving credit where it's due, and including others in your fun (e.g., including the new engineer when you go for coffee) make life better for everyone. I find that smiling, acknowledging other people's struggles ("man, that sounds tough!"), and cracking the occasional G-rated joke go a long way too, particularly when there's tension to resolve.

- **Seek out others' opinions**: You depend on your colleagues' expertise, and you want them to know you value it—they'll share their thoughts more liberally as well as enjoy your collaboration more. Asking for their thoughts explicitly, both in private and in public, is a vote of respect and a strong compliment. Obviously you need to weigh that compliment against the drain on others' time; I consider it especially valuable with junior colleagues who may assume that you don't value their input.

- **Leave when it's time to leave**: I can't count the times I've had someone come into my office and start talking— someone I like and respect and am eager to share a word with—and then had them keep talking while I become progressively more desperate to get back to work. I don't know if it's a universal issue or a sickness specific to engineering, but it is a problem. My advice is to err toward leaving people to get back to work quickly, and especially to keep your eyes open for cues that people are done—shortened responses, half-turning in a different direction, and seeming antsy. You can always say, "catch up with you later" and make your exit.

- **Acknowledge struggle; be supportive**: Like every job, engineering is filled with moments of frustration. People can become quite emotional when their project is canceled, they cause an outage, their favorite colleague leaves, or whatever else goes wrong. For me, it's can be powerful when someone just asks, "how are you doing after that reorg?" or says, after I struggled to resolve an outage, "don't worry about it, you did your best"; that support builds trust and mutual caring. Ref: Forget Feedback and Provide Support below.

Humility vs. Self-deprecation

I've worked with quite a few people who feel outclassed by their teammates; they see smart, experienced people all around them, and they feel that they're behind and will never catch up. Respecting your teammates is a virtue, but I've seen many engineers manifest that admiration as constant self-deprecation: comments like "I have no idea what's going on" or "I don't think I should be making this decision." Humility is a virtue, and so is esteem for one's colleagues, but bringing yourself down is not professionalism—if you tell people you don't belong in the big leagues, your attitude is proving it to be the truth, and they'll believe it, because your colleagues know that deep technical work requires at least some trust in yourself. I advise against insulting yourself at work. Remember that everyone feels dread and self-doubt; we can share it with our friends, but at work we should keep our chins up.

Delivering Feedback

Finding fault isn't a recreational sport, and we do our best to praise rather than criticize. However, sometimes people need to hear feedback; sometimes we're the person to deliver it. This section will discuss when and how to deliver criticism. These principles are derived from my many misadventures in feedback with teams on three continents, and I've been happy with the results of following them. Remember, however, that expectations around feedback, and especially directness, vary across cultures and individuals; you'll have to do your best to adapt to your own team's context.

When

Feedback is a gift, but giving it is a risk; sometimes people will love you for going out on a limb to help them improve, and sometimes they'll resent you. You'll disagree with how people do things all the time, but because of this risk, you should often do nothing, especially when the consequences are minor (and therefore the upside small). There are three main situations when I'll give people constructive feedback.

- I'm in a position of authority, seniority, or friendship to them, and I think that the feedback will help them succeed personally; in that case, I have a responsibility to help them improve.

- The behavior in question significantly compromises our shared work; in that case, giving feedback may be a practical necessity.

- The criticism is mild and the benefit is large. For example, I may think that a colleague can make a tiny tweak to their presentation style for a big benefit; in that case, I may be able to deliver the feedback as encouragement and run minimal risk.

And these opportunities do arise—I've given peers and reports feedback on their communication, on their discipline, on bringing negativity to the office, on their sense of ownership, and on and on. Usually, I take the plunge out of a spirit of friendship or because I genuinely believe in people's potential, and usually (not always) they've in the end come back to thank me; the right frequency is more than never. Once I have given some feedback, I'll wait until the dust settles to deliver the next round; too much feedback at a time will exhaust even the most open-hearted colleague.

Foundational Principles of Giving Feedback

I think there are two key principles to effective feedback. They don't guarantee success, but they're better than nothing:

1. **Give people the benefit of the doubt**: And tell them that you do. Assume that they mean well, that they're trying hard, and that they want to be the best they can be, and tell them that you're giving them feedback because you believe they mean well.

2. **Give feedback in the most positive way you can**: Approach conversations with an earnest goal of helping them succeed for their own sake, starting from respect and optimism rather than contempt or anger.

You can apply those principles in a million creative ways to find the feedback most likely to succeed in a given situation, but I'll suggest a few techniques that have given me a lot of mileage.

Empathy; Show Your Trust

Feedback lands softer if it comes with understanding. When you see well-intentioned people messing up, you can usually guess why—maybe they're gentle people snapping because they're stressed out, maybe they're disorganized this week because they have too much on their plate, maybe their code isn't up to snuff because they don't know the language well or don't understand the expectations for the system they're changing. You can be explicit that you think the lapse is understandable and why, and by doing so, show that you feel no contempt, only respect.

Suppose Kate just took Steve to task in a meeting for coming unprepared. The feedback does need to be given, but we think the intensity was too high. We want Kate to take a milder tone next time; we give some meta-feedback.

So-so:

You were too tough on Steve in there; why did you talk to him like that?

Good:

I think that you may have been too harsh with Steve in that meeting. I was also pretty frustrated that he didn't come prepared, and I completely agree that he needs to know that he has to do better for this project to succeed. That said, I think he might respond better if we approach him a little more gently.

Kate most likely didn't go to town on Steve for fun; she wants this project to succeed, and it's stressful and frustrating that her colleague didn't come through. She may be embarrassed about her behavior already. We let her know what we think, but we also show that we find her behavior natural and relatable under the circumstances; we're not remotely contemptuous.

Acknowledge What's Good

You've probably heard of the unfortunately named "shit sandwich"—delivering criticism surrounded by praise to buttress someone's ego. Ben Horowitz says in *The Hard Thing About Hard Things* that people see right through it, and it's certainly risky—any stretch of honesty is more likely to backfire than help. I personally think some judicious honest praise can indeed lift someone's spirits if it's contextually relevant; you should be helping your recipient see real reasons to counterweight the disappointment they'll feel at having erred. That means that the praise needs to be tightly coupled to the feedback, and it goes without saying that it should be honest—if not it will be much worse than nothing.

A non sequitur to be seen through:

You've done such great coding work this week! I just want to mention one thing that I think should be tweaked in the presentation.

An effective contextually relevant compliment:

I think the sections about reliability and performance are clear and persuasive. The section on implementation details is well done, but I think might be too much for this audience.

In the former, we're clearly buttering someone up; the compliment is off-topic. In the latter, we're commenting holistically on the work, including positive things to feel good about and areas for improvement; the compliment is truthful and fully relevant and can therefore be taken seriously.

Phrase Feedback As an Opportunity

This is a phrasing optimization that can make criticism subtly more palatable; rather than saying, "you need to do X" or "you shouldn't do Y" or "Z is wrong," we can say, "I think if you do X, <something favorable will happen>".

For example, the following is direct and useful feedback: "you need to add an introduction or the rest will be hard to follow." The same feedback can land a little better as, "I think that the main technical sections are good, but if you add a clear introduction, readers may contextualize them better." The effect is subtle, but to me this phrasing makes it clear that we're working together to a common goal rather than fault-finding.

Qualify Your Certainty

"Knowing Our Limits" (Chapter 7) discusses the elusiveness of certainty in the software game and the importance of explicitness about our level of confidence in a theory. When delivering feedback, expressing certainty increases the intensity for the victim.

A touch intense (and maybe unreasonably self-assured):

You need to cover more of the history in your doc.

Properly qualified:

How much does your audience know about the history of this system? Depending on what they know, I think the doc might benefit from a little more history.

These two sentences deliver the same message; the first is certain and therefore commanding and final; it's a little slap in the face, a wake-up call and a debate finisher. The second is milder and less certain, an open door for discussion, debate and encouragement; you acknowledge that your colleague, whose judgment you respect, may have good reasons for a decision you prima facie disagree with, and you even offer a potential justification for their decision (maybe their audience does know the history).

You might well use the first occasionally, when your colleague needs a wake-up call, but I'll always default to the second, and I think this acknowledgment that you may be wrong sets the stage for a supportive discussion.

Offer Help

Another way to help your colleagues receive feedback is to couple it with an offer of help; you're showing therefore that you're not just raining criticism and leaving them to struggle but that you really want to help them succeed. For example:

I think the postmortem might need a bit more detail about how the caching system works.

---

vs.

I think the postmortem might need a bit more detail about how the caching subsystem works.
Are you familiar with it? If you like, I'd be happy to spend a few minutes talking over some of the quirks.

The feedback is of course the same, but the second is an open hand; you're instantly in it together, an instant comfort for someone struggling with a difficult problem or perhaps embarrassed that they needed constructive feedback.

Deliver Feedback 1:1

This is a well-known method. While there can be good reasons to give feedback publicly, especially for a manager who's trying to create a culture of candor, that requires a deft touch; it's safer to deliver your feedback 1:1, in person or by a direct email, where you save your colleague the risk of public embarrassment (especially if your tone isn't spot on).

Manage Your Tone of Voice

This one is a hard theory to convey on the printed page, but note: feedback stings when delivered with a vehement, staccato tone. When someone you like is doing something poorly, you may be frustrated with them—your earnest desire to help them may be mixed with frustration, and that can come through and hurt. Do your very best to find a mild, easy, friendly tone. You'll see that this is just an extension into voice of all the themes above—trying to make yourself a friend to people enduring the tough business of receiving criticism.

Forget Feedback and Provide Support

I was once on a team whose manager had left, and no one was getting the close air support they needed from the second-level manager. As the most senior engineer on the team, I was trying to maintain a sense of normalcy (and keep the team together) during that tough period. One day, a colleague I held in very high regard said something quite snippy in our team meeting about how we'd been X months without a manager. I was, momentarily, livid; this was a senior person who should have been helping his colleagues cope, not spreading discontent, and I expected more of him. I was about to take him aside and give him a piece of my mind, when something else occurred to me.

The reason I expected more of him was that he was a great engineer and a strong professional; so why had he acted out? My conclusion was that he must have been in a dark place himself; maybe criticism would be justified, but maybe support would get better results.

I asked him: "are you okay? You seemed kind of upset in that meeting." And, indeed, he had been. We talked about what he'd been feeling and why things had been tough recently—I think that was the first step toward what became a treasured professional relationship. So, sometimes, nurture is the better part of valor.

Tough Love

Finally, we come to the last tool in the toolbox: tough love, direct statements that we know may upset their target. I save them almost exclusively for situations where I think intransigence is going to cause real harm, in every case as a last resort:

1. When stubbornness seems to be about to cause a business-critical mistake.

2. When friends' seem likely to do themselves and others a significant disservice.

The business risk case speaks more or less for itself. If I give feedback gently and it isn't followed, I'll usually just let it slide—the upside usually isn't worth the friction. If failure is simply not an option, for example, during an ongoing system outage, I won't hesitate to use a strong tone and words to get things on track; for example, I've many times raised my voice to stop people from talking over each other during an outage. Set in a loud, unamused voice: "everyone stop and mute. I want to hear from Uday and no one else." That's something I would never say under normal circumstances, but when seconds matter, we impose ourselves as we have to. I'll almost always circle back after the fact to apologize for being forceful and explain why it was necessary.

Similarly, if I feel that a system design decision is a real business risk, I'll first try every gentle method in my book, but if that fails, I will absolutely say, "this decision is an unacceptable risk; we have to do better."

The case of friendship is more delicate. We break out the tough love toolbox with friends for nonbusiness reasons: because we want the best for them where we might just let others make their mistakes. Once again, we try every gentle tool first, and even when forced to be direct, we'll do our best to encourage. But, we will be direct. Said in real life to a friend who had a plan to give an ultimatum to their boss:

I don't think saying that to your boss is going to get good results; I think he'll experience it to mean that you're no longer on the same side working toward a common goal, and that is not going to incline him to help you achieve what you want to achieve. I'm telling you this because I think it's important and I think you can handle the feedback and do better.

Receiving Feedback

I have only three pieces of advice for receiving feedback: seek it out often, do your best to receive it with an open mind, and express appreciation whether you agree or not.

You should seek out feedback because it is a precious currency, a rare opportunity to use insightful people's judgment to improve yourself or your work. I think asking for feedback can be a casual business to be done quite often, and in fact, asking is a show of respect—it can be a way to build a relationship. I suggest that you ask the most specific question you can. "Do you have any feedback for me?" can be a good show of humility, and you never know, you might catch something when you go fishing. However, to busy experts, more specific questions feel more intelligent and more actionable. "Do you mind reading this email and seeing if it's clear for this audience?" "Do you have any feedback on my presentation? I'd appreciate a second opinion." "Do you think my question was reasonable in that meeting?"

As we've discussed at length, giving feedback is a risk, and doing so is an act of generosity—the delivery may be annoying, the feedback may be wrong, but your colleague is trying to help, and you should do your best to give an honest thanks. Almost everyone naturally becomes annoyed and defensive—crush those impulses, find your maturity, and say "thank you."

Completely apart from that, you should try to consider the feedback with the greatest openness you can. You might conclude that you disagree completely, and you might be right, but you should do your best to reflect on it; you may see wisdom in it after you recover from the initial shock of criticism.

Working With Your Manager

This section will discuss how to get the best results from your collaboration with your boss. We'll start by offering a model for the relationship that underpins everything else. Then, we'll cover the responsibilities and psychology of managers themselves, so you can model your boss' own problems and motivations and optimize your collaboration. Finally, we'll discuss what to do when things go wrong.

The Nature of the Relationship

One fact threads through every aspect of working with your manager: your interaction is above all a business relationship. Your Relationship With Your Employer (Chapter 1) argues that you should view your interaction with your employer dispassionately but not cynically; you deliver on your commitments, they deliver on theirs, and you both profit. Managers are representatives of the company, imbued with special authority over people and budget and special responsibility to the shareholders and the law—for example, managers in the United States have a special legal responsibility to act if they become aware of harassment. In fact, you can consider them personifications of the company, and you should have much the same expectations of them that you have of your employer overall.

Luckily, within the company, your interests are usually aligned. Success on your projects is good for your manager, and they usually want to see you rewarded, even at the expense of other teams, because they want their team members to stay happy and stay put.

Your interaction with your boss is also, unavoidably, personal—you see a lot of each other, and since your interests are aligned, you'll struggle together to achieve the same ends. Their power over you and responsibility for you can also make them feel, sometimes (terribly misleadingly), like a parent. Sometimes you'll love each other, and sometimes you'll drive each other nuts. Like all good business relationships, you should enjoy a mutual respect and a degree of friendship, but we should organize our behavior around its nonpersonal core. Managers are obliged to maintain a professional distance from their reports; you shouldn't expect your boss to be your close friend, to see you socially, or, especially, to party with you.

As in any business relationship, we should respect ourselves and our partners, keep our cool, and express our opinions honestly and courteously. It's natural to be afraid of your boss when you start (see On Fear, Confusion, and Self-Loathing: Starting New Jobs), but they're quite unlikely to summarily fire you, and your fear of them will fade. We don't need to abase ourselves before our boss, and they should never ask us to; we should respect their position of responsibility, and they should return that respect. We should never expect them to do anything out of sentiment, and we should never expect a sense of entitlement to get us anywhere.

Finally, we should pretty much do what our boss tells us to do to the extent that ethics allow. Many engineers have been infected, in today's talent seller's market, with the false impression that they don't need to listen to their managers. It's true that you're paid to exercise discretion; you should represent your opinions faithfully and even, in extremely rare cases, go over your manager's head if you believe they are putting the company at risk. But, in the end, their job is to guide you in doing what the company needs, and your job is to do what they say, even when you don't like it.

Managers Have Their Own Problems: Optimizing the Collaboration

Managers are accountable for goals—shipping software, maintaining reliability, and driving business metrics. They have project managers pinging them constantly, their own boss breathing down their neck, and an eye always forward to annual review season, when, it may surprise you to hear, they usually want to be able to get you the best review and compensation possible—which might require a knockdown drag-out fight with other managers.

And yet, they do almost none of the work with their own hands. Therefore, despite their authority over you, they suffer from a peculiar disempowerment: the main way they can get projects done is to sit back and let you do your job. You can probably see how this creates a temptation to micromanage—everyone wants, in their hearts, to be able to do something to influence their fate.

All of which tells you that the most important thing you can for your relationship with your manager is give them (justified) confidence that you are going to come through for them—help them wait comfortably, rather than anxiously, for you to come through. I suggest three ways to do that, one obvious, two less so.

The most important thing you can do, by far, is build a track record of delivering—the more you deliver, the more confidence your manager will have next time. Fine, we are done with the obvious.

Second, proactive, well-organized communication about project status helps put your manager at ease. If you come to team meetings and 1:1s with a list of project areas and a clear story for each, and you deliver that story with authority, you show that you're on top of things. You can use the email template for project status updates (Chapter 13) to structure both email and in-person updates. Everyone wants to make a better workplace for introverts, but I still advise you to tell your story decisively, speaking firmly and at medium volume—conveying confidence builds confidence. Similarly, if you surface project risks and schedule slips the moment you're aware of them, you let your manager rest easy that there are no surprises lurking around the corner.

Finally, managers love engineers who find a way. At senior levels, discretion and strategy are prized, but for junior engineers, getting things done (at reasonable quality) is more or less the beginning of the end. If you show that you won't get blocked, that you'll Just Do Something (Chapter 5) rather than let a project ever languish, you're off and running.

Upward Feedback

Sometimes, your manager has a problem and needs to hear about it; maybe team meetings are too slow, maybe there's a technical problem that needs more attention, maybe you're being micromanaged. When you have an idea for how your team or manager can improve, you should (often) provide that feedback; it's good for you, it's good for your team, and when done right, managers will often (not always) respect and appreciate it. This is just a special case of delivering feedback, but (a) it's scarier, and (b) the long-running nature of your relationship requires extra care.

Here are three things to keep in mind:

1. Your manager is a person too, and they can be wounded just like anyone, which will make them less open to your feedback. Express minimal anger or frustration, and don't get personal; remember, this is work, not family. Try to make a specific, actionable request or suggestion. So, avoid the personal attack, even if it's true:

You've been micromanaging me, and it's really frustrating me.

Prefer an emotionally neutral, actionable proposal for improving your work together:

I've appreciated that you're staying very tuned in to what's happening on this project, but I've been thinking that it might be good to batch our communication a bit to reduce the overhead. Would you be open to a brief daily summary email at the end of the day?

---

2. Pace yourself. When you work together constantly, you'll see many opportunities for feedback; too much at a time will make them feel beaten down and less receptive to you. Prioritize and trickle it out.

3. Pay attention to the response; if they become defensive, ease off the gas and save it for another day.

Going Over Your Manager's Head

Going over your manager's head (raising a concern about them directly with their boss) is a drastic measure; it harms your trust with your manager, likely irreparably, and, if not well justified, your second-level manager will have their own doubts about your judgment. Mere disagreement isn't a reason to take this step. If you don't agree with your boss' direction or methods, your first thought should always be direct feedback. If that doesn't work, you can always switch teams or quit without burning any bridges. You should only go over your manager's head when (a) direct feedback either hasn't worked or seems impossible and (b) they are doing something so injurious to the company's interests that you consider it a near emergency, something their boss desperately needs to know about. That situation has virtually never happened to me, but it does happen; at that time, you can reach out to your second-level manager and express your concerns with the same unemotional professionalism you would employ for direct feedback.

Tricky Subjects

You're going to have challenges with your boss at some point, something between mild technical disagreement, which requires you to either persuade them or get over it, and harassment, which may require you to consult HR or a lawyer. This section will offer approaches to a few tricky issues that can arise in engineer–manager relationships. In almost every case, you can try to work with your manager to improve the situation. Also in almost every case—apart from illegal or discriminatory conduct—if that doesn't work, your main options are to find your peace with it or move on. As emergency fallbacks for illegal behavior or terrible business risks (as opposed to simpler frustrations), you can go either up the chain or to HR.

Disagreement About Technology or Process

When you take issue with your team's practices or technical direction, you have two choices: you can keep it to yourself, or you can offer constructive feedback.

"I think you're prioritizing wrong" is whiny. Get traction with concrete feedback that doesn't reference to individual qualities: "I've been thinking we might want to consider <doing X instead of Y>. X <has benefits>, but Y <has other benefits>." For example:

I think we might want to prioritize the monitoring cleanup ahead of the UI. The UI is going to be a great product improvement, but right now, the on-call burden is really slowing people down, and we could improve morale a lot with just 2 engineer-weeks of work.

Remember that a mild approach (not putting people on the defensive) and a convincing argument are your sharpest tools.

You Want More Feedback

When I started my first job, my manager didn't give me any feedback for the first six months or so—not a single word that I can recall. Since I was neurotically fixated on getting terminated, this let me get pretty worked up, to the point that my anxiety obstructed my work. Since, I've realized that if you're not sure where you stand, you can just directly ask for feedback! In fact, it can come off quite well, as a sign of humility and eagerness to improve. I'd advise you to suggest a specific feedback cadence. For example,

---

I've been thinking that it could be beneficial for me get some more feedback on my work. Do you think we could try to have a regular cadence of feedback? It doesn't need to be too heavyweight—maybe once every two weeks, or once a month, you could give me some feedback?

If you're not sure, one good way to structure feedback is as two observations: one about what you've done well and one about what you've done poorly. That structure ensures at least some constructive feedback, but it balances the criticism with encouragement.

Slow Advancement

I hear from many engineers that they think they're ready for promotion, and it hasn't happened. This section will offer several options for approaching that problem; note that this analysis does not apply to scenarios of discrimination or harassment, which may be best discussed with HR or an employment lawyer. You should approach the issue of promotion cautiously, because perceived entitlement can grate on managers.

Personally, I don't think this is a subject we should "be on top of" all the time; we should focus all our energy on (a) improving ourselves and (b) finding and executing on awesome projects, which is by far the shortest, straightest shot to a promotion. That said, sometimes, we need to be proactive.

I would broach this subject from the perspective of "making a career plan" with your boss. You can say, "I'd like to talk about my goals for the next year," and then, in that discussion, say, "I'm starting to think about promotion to Level X. What do you think I should do to position myself for that? How do you think I'm doing against that standard?"

This is a perfectly acceptable subject for discussion; there's nothing tasteless or entitled about a career strategy session and a request for feedback, and you may well learn a lot about where your manager thinks you stand. Of course, if you're laughably underperforming, it won't come off great, but if you think you are on track, it's a graceful opening to the conversation.

If your manager responds that they think you aren't on track, and you disagree, I suggest you start by assuming your manager is right and thinking carefully about their feedback. Of course, some managers are wrong about everything, but there's a better-than-50–50 chance you're getting ahead of yourself; you can also try to get a consistency check from a senior colleague, emphasizing that you appreciate candor.

If you conclude that you are being held back, I'll offer three options.

You can be patient: If your boss says that you just need to wait a little longer (e.g., "in six months I think we can make a good case"), and your situation is otherwise good, I'd encourage you to just play it cool. Good learning and work you care about are worth more than a quick promotion. You can set a time limit for this approach and reevaluate after that time.

You can have a direct, professional conversation with your manager: What you should say is, "I've been thinking about my timeline for promotion. I respect what you've told me about this, but if you don't mind, I want to make a case that I'm ready sooner than we've discussed." Then, you can talk about why you think your promotion is justified. You should make that case calmly, be ostentatiously humble, and phrase your case precisely in terms of the work you do and the promotion criteria at your company.

"I work so hard," "I think this is really unfair," or, "why don't you want to support me" are childish arguments that offer no information or logic, and they'll annoy a businessperson with the tough responsibility of allocating promotions and budget.

On the other hand, if you tell them about work they may not know about, reveal complexity they may not understand, or clarify your execution against the company standards, you may impress with your professionalism and persuade with your logic. The following is an example of a direct, fact-based argument that avoids entitlement with an explicit show of humility.

I think that on Project X, I needed to step into a leadership role that's appropriate for Level Y. That was a virtual team with four junior people, and they needed a lot of guidance; I also did all the project management, including sending the updates and maintaining the tracker, and the project shipped on time. The Level Y guidelines say that you need to be able to coordinate projects of two to three engineers. I thought that it may not have been obvious externally, because it was a virtual team, but this work met that standard. Of course, I understand that the promotion process might be more nuanced than I realized. What do you think?

You can quietly, responsibly leave: If your manager is truly unfair and intransigent, then this is your best option. If you do, you should never say that was because you couldn't get promoted; that's a bitter departure for no discernible benefit.

Project Dissatisfaction

Every career involves a certain amount of biting the bullet and doing boring, painful work. If you never swallow your pride and do the grunt work, you don't deserve the good stuff; good work should, and usually does, go to team players who show that they won't quit when things get boring.

That said, your career also can't only be taking one for the team—good engineers want to feel the wind in their hair, and you deserve a chance to take on fun, ambitious projects. So, if you've been turning the crank for too long, how do you ask for a chance to do something more fun?

The first step is to make it extremely clear that you're going to deliver your current work and that you understand you're not entitled to just do whatever your heart desires. Then, you can ask about the future. You should prepare the most specific idea you can (sometimes that will be a very specific project, sometimes an area, etc.) and justify it in terms of business value.

We're almost getting to the end of Project Jellybean. I've been thinking about what comes next after we've shipped. I'd really like to do a performance project if that's possible; I think we have a lot of low-hanging fruit for performance, and it may improve the customer experience a lot.

If you get stuck in a rut despite giving input about your interests, you can be (cautiously) direct, still without whining:

My last two projects have been a lot of plumbing. I think they added a lot of business value, and I'm glad to have done them, but I think I could use a change of pace soon—do you think I could tackle some infrastructure work when we finish Project Gumdrop?

If none of that gets you where you need to be, remember that you can always move on: see "Maintenance Is for Suckers" in Chapter 4.

Working with Platform Owners

Platforms are software components used by many clients—a storage system, a widely used library, a networking layer, a build system, etc., etc. This can be compared to, say, a tool maintained in common by one team and used only by that team.

You're going to collaborate with platform owners, and you're going to want things from them; both require a special sensitivity to those teams' position. This section will discuss how to get the most out of those collaborations.

The first thing to remember about platform teams is that their responsibilities are, by definition, broad—they have obligations to many users, most of whom are not you. They get tons of questions every day, many of them ignorant and answerable by reading a wiki; they get tons of feature requests, most either asinine or beneficial to only a single customer; they get constant complaints about "bugs" that are really misuse.

You'll collaborate most fruitfully with platform teams when you do the exact opposite of those things—show that you respect the difficulties of their job, defer to their superior knowledge, and above all take full responsibility for your own success. Then, you can build a partnership where their expertise and your feedback improve both teams' results.

Here's how that looks.

Feature Requests

A good feature request is decorated with abundant context.

First, it should be framed in terms of what you want to achieve rather than how it should be done. For example, "Feature Request: a way to query a store's most recent orders," rather than "include recent orders in getStore API." The latter is prescriptive; it implies that you know the best way to achieve your goals with your colleague's platform, and it also doesn't give them enough information to offer alternatives. The former gives them the whole picture. Sure, sometimes you truly need a tweak to a specific API, but even then, you should describe your needs at the highest level you can.

Second, it should explain the business purpose of your request. For example, "we want to add a view of the most recent orders to the Store View page on the site." This helps your audience reason about alternatives and weigh the priority of your request. If you want the data for analytics or for a call to order, you might have very different requirements than if it's for showing a real-time view to store owners.

Third, you should describe any and all relevant technical context, again to empower an informed response without the need for follow-up questions.

Finally, it should be expressed humbly. This is as simple as acknowledging that the team may be busy or that your request may not be viable.

Here's an example to put it all together:

Feature Request: a way to query a store's most recent orders.

We're building a call to order on the store view. We're hoping to show a near real-time view of the most recent orders in the user's area. It's not important that the data be extremely fresh, but the fresher the better for greater truthfulness. Currently, we get all the store data from the getStore API. We're not sure whether the store service currently has access to this information, or if so, what the right API to expose it would be; if it's quite tricky, please let us know, and we can meet to discuss how best to get the data. Thanks!

Debugging and Technical Questions

The two keys to getting help from a platform owner are

Going deep before you ask: Plenty of people come to a platform team and say, things aren't working the way I expect, please help. Model clients aren't afraid to go deep on their own; they read the docs, they read the code, they look at logs, they look at graphs, they try several things, and generally they act like a service owner themselves; they ask for help only when they're fairly confident that (a) they aren't doing anything wrong themselves and (b) going further on their own would be wasteful.

Asking clear, context-rich questions: See the debugging question template in Chapter 14. If you omit context or ask an unclear question, you're blending in with an annoying herd. A well-framed question starts you on the right foot.

Bug Reports

The standards for bug reports are very similar to those for feature requests. The structure should always be

- What I'm trying to achieve

- Exactly what I did, always including real commands or example requests, real version numbers or git hashes, and every possible bit of context

- Exactly what I expected to see

- Exactly what I saw, including real copy–pasted output.

- Ideally, some attempt at debugging the issue

For example:

---

getStore API returns HTTP 500 if store is closed and user requests details.

I expect to be able to fetch stores even when they are closed. If I request the base store, this seems to work fine. However, if I also request details, I see a 5XX. For example, my test store, dhs-bookstore, is always closed.

```
$ curl https://stores-site.com/api/v1/stores/dhs-bookstore
| jq --compact-output {"name":"dhs-bookstore", "status":"closed", ... }
```

Works fine, but

```
$ curl -v \https://stores-site.com/api/v1/stores/dhs-
bookstore?details=true

...
HTTP/1.1 500 Internal Server Error
```

It looks to me like this error is coming from the processOutput function, line 121, which doesn't handle a null "inflight orders" field.

The importance of copying your real commands and real output can't be overstated; good debuggers are too experienced with misleading questions to trust anything else (see the "Magic Question Templates" in Chapter 14).

Shining in an Engineering Organization

In the last chapter, you learned about fruitful collaboration with individuals. This chapter will broaden that analysis to a whole organization: practices to make you an ideal citizen of your team, maximizing your value to your company while building credibility and appreciation among your teammates. In addition to universally applicable practices, I'll touch on the delicate subject of politics—getting things done in the presence of controversy.

Reputation and Personal Brand

The power of a good reputation is probably intuitive to you: that people want to work with you, that they listen to your ideas, that they trust you with important work, and that they give you the benefit of the doubt for advancement.

I'm here to tell that, luckily, you don't need to do anything special to build a good reputation; you don't need to brand yourself, tweet, or blog (unless you like the buzz of being a pundit). I posit: steadily doing good work and treating people right are enough to build a good reputation. If you deliver your

© Daniel Heller 2020

D. Heller, *Building a Career in Software*, https://doi.org/10.1007/978-1-4842-6147-7_7

projects, write good code, document it well for others, step forward to help teammates, and shut your mouth when you have the urge to say something unkind, people are going to grow to respect you. Doing those things every day is no walk in the park, but that's what we aspire to, not just because it's right but because if a good reputation is "easily" earned by steadily doing the right thing, then a good reputation is just as easily lost with a tantrum or a responsibility shirked.

One thing that can help you get your name out there is becoming the go-to person for some technology. Again, this is actually a simple problem that doesn't need a special solution: if you seek out projects based on impact and enjoyment, you'll naturally go deep enough to become an area expert, and then people will learn your name and come to you for help. So don't sweat it. Find the impact and the fun.

Helpfulness

A colleague from another team, visibly stressed, once asked me to add a snippet of kernel code to support a security feature he was building. It seemed reasonable to me, so I replied, "sure, when do you need it by?" He seemed overcome with relief; the same day, he went to my manager to sing my praises. He'd been under deadline, and several engineers had refused to help him; I've never seen clearer proof that it's an overwhelming relief for anyone to have a colleague take a serious interest in helping them succeed and that there's no easier way for you to make a friend and ally.

You should help colleagues every chance you get—not grudgingly, but enthusiastically, hustling when they need something fast, digging if you don't know an answer off the top of your head, taking an interest in their deadlines and frustrations, apologizing if you accidentally go slower than you could, connecting them to others when you can. The foremost reason is because it's the right thing to do; you're making the workplace you want to be a part of. If you need a practical reason, it's because the goodwill you earn is large compared to the effort you spend. You should adjust depending on your own commitments, but your default position should be to help full throttle.

Running Toward Fires

A corollary to that personal helpfulness is running toward fires—taking your team's problems as your own. When your team's software has an outage, your tests break, or users are hitting some kind of bug, you should almost always take the interrupt and lean in to help. I've never understood why people *don't* do this—my suspicion is not laziness but timidity, a fear of seeming too loud or aggressive—because (a) it's clearly the right thing to do and (b) it's an easy way to build a brand as a responsible owner and go-to person in your area. It doesn't matter if you know how to fix a problem the instant you hear about it—you can *try*; you just might get somewhere, and people are all but guaranteed to appreciate it.

Politics and Political Capital

"Politics" in business is the exercise of influence by social methods—persuasion, coercion, and favor trading. It also has a special usage for a misalignment of interests: when two people can't both get what they want and try to attain their respective goals by influence on others.

Politics spans a spectrum from necessary to Game of Thrones.

At the "necessary" end are campaigns for good ideas, like explaining an important idea 1:1 to several people to marshal support a valuable business decision. Though it's purely advocacy on the strength of an idea's merits, I would still call this "politics" for its social dimension—it requires understanding whose support is necessary for an idea to succeed, reasoning about how to persuade them, and connecting with them.

At the "evil" end are treacheries like slandering someone to an executive or killing a valuable project by quietly withholding a tiny bit of necessary support—duplicity and pursuing your own interests at the expense of the greater good.

The Necessary Form

Engineers use the term "politics" almost exclusively pejoratively—we think good ideas should win on their merits and are suspicious of social maneuvering. In fact, we need to practice the mild form of politics to execute on big ideas, because they always require big decisions (by leaders) and the support of many teams and individuals. In very short summary, this kind of politics is about marshaling the strongest goodwill and support you can for an idea by honest, proactive, emotionally intelligent effort to persuade others. When *you* need to get something done, keep in mind the following.

Understand who makes decisions. For example, recognizing that the manager on a team may look to their tech lead when making a decision and that you need to persuade not just the manager but the tech lead as well.

See what matters to other stakeholders in a decision, and understand how your idea may benefit or harm them; identify compromises that may balance those concerns for various people involved. For example, recognizing that migrating onto your new platform, which will simplify *your* life, will cost a significant amount of effort for a partner team but that if they do so, their operational load should be reduced, honestly acknowledging the cost while emphasizing the benefits.

Reason about what different audiences know and don't know, and find the best way to communicate your ideas to them (e.g., a senior engineer may need a different language than an executive).

Recognize who may be inconvenienced or harmed by a decision and how to restore their support. For example, expressing honest sympathy for someone whose project has been delayed or canceled in favor of yours and trying to help them get excited about what they can contribute to your project.

Understand the strength of our own standing, or *political capital,* and therefore how vigorously you need to persuade and when you can simply dictate or assert.

Political Capital

The last of these, political capital, bears more discussion. Political capital is the trust of decision-makers (including coders making decisions only about themselves); people's inclination to do what you say and tell others to do the same, because they trust you. Political capital is built more or less one way: by taking on problems and getting results. It's a bank account: we deposit by delivering business value and building others' trust, and we withdraw by asking others to spend energy, money, or their own political capital based on our advice—when things go well, we get back more capital than spend, but when we fail, we might lose our investment.

The principle of the use of political capital is to match the exercise of authority to our credibility. This is the tricky, subtle, no-rule-book-exists art of figuring out who trusts us and how much they're willing to bet on our advice and asking neither too much (more than people are willing to bet based on their trust) nor too little (getting too little done because we underestimate how much people will listen to us). Managers, executives, peers, and subordinates will do what you say to the extent that

(a) They believe that you're saying the right things.

(b) They like you personally, that is, they want to.

(c) You're backed by real authority, that is, they have to.

(a) and (b) are our preferred methods; they cause the least strain and produce the most vigorous effort, because people are happy to do the right thing for people they like. That's why persuasion is our number one tool, but persuasion depends on credibility as well as on eloquence—if people don't trust you to get results, they'll be less receptive to your message. If your message is compelling but the scale of the undertaking is enormous, and your trust is only medium, people still won't follow you—they may think you're right, but they need to trust you more to bet the farm.

So, we're always assessing: How much are people willing to bet on me? I only know of two ways to assess that—asking for feedback ("how do you think people will respond to this?") and listening carefully to see how people do in fact respond to us—do they ask for our opinion? Do they loop us in to important discussions?

You'll also encounter people whose interests are strongly aligned against the Right Thing to Do—for example, a team who owns a system that has many problems and needs to be replaced but will lose their mission if that system is deprecated. You should still do your very best to persuade, and even people whose tactical interests are harmed often respond to the big picture story.

When they don't is when you can use your capital to draw on authority from leaders; if you've built the trust of people with real authority, you can ask them to tell people what to do, and they will. It's a tool to be used very carefully, both because it costs them too (they'd much rather persuade than order!) and because an order is an easy way to alienate a team—both imply that the payoff needs to be large and that you need a lot of capital to take the plunge.

The Evil Form

Politics are inevitable; people's ideas and interests will conflict, and they will represent those interests the best they can. The evil formulation either puts the interests of the individual ahead of those of the enterprise (e.g., trying to kill a good idea because it diminishes your influence) or draws on evil methods: bullying or dishonesty. In my own experience, treachery is rare in software—we're just not that sophisticated—but I have had people steal credit for my work and bad-mouth me in public.

I wish I had a recipe for defense against those tactics, but I don't—they're hard to detect and hard to respond to without seeming petty yourself. My only advice is to fall back on honesty, evangelism, and hard work yourself—good public speaking, good writing, and good results seem to win in the long run. You can calmly raise concerns with superiors, though you can never whine. If you get to the point where the stakes are high and treachery matters, you're probably beyond the scope of this book and should be reading about how to become an executive.

Professionals Maximize Business Value: In Which Open Source is Stealing From the Shareholders... Sometimes

Let's start this section with some controversy: open source work on company time is sometimes thievery. It's work motivated by technical enthusiasm, personal open-source brand, love of free software, preparation for starting a separate company, virtually anything except what engineers are overpaid to do: adding business value. Actually, I think the modern explosion of open-source software is a miracle that we should treasure—but I will still use it to illustrate how engineers fail as professionals and should reconsider how we evaluate our time.

As a knowledge worker, to paraphrase Peter Drucker, you are an "executive"; you exercise discretion over your own time and budget (e.g., salary) to maximize business value. In fact, somewhere out there, real people—investors—have put their trust in you to faithfully represent their interests, a commitment we should take as seriously as an attorney takes their fiduciary commitment to a client.

I've always felt that responsibility; I'm infamous for unfunny quips about "going back to adding shareholder value" after coffee breaks. I recently came to see this issue much more clearly, when a company I worked at had an IPO. My friend Shuby told me that she had invested, and I felt a stab of anxiety—Shuby had put her faith in me (and others) to treat her money with care, to do my best to grow it, so that she could use that money to someday buy a house or send her kids to school.

Shuby is a real person! But there are hundreds of thousands (or millions) out there like her. Ever since, I can't help but think, "do it for Shuby,"[1] when I'm staring down a tough problem, weighing how much to spend on a business trip, or even deciding what to do when I get into the office.

So, we come back to open source. For some companies, like Google with Kubernetes or DataStax with Cassandra, open source is a critical part of their business strategy. If that's your situation, well, go nuts. However, if you're working on closed-source software and deciding whether to agitate for open sourcing it, your position should be no, unless you see the clear business value. The reason is that maintaining an open source project takes a lot of time and focus ("it fails on Debian Jessie!" "It doesn't work when I run it under a debugger!", etc.), reduces your freedom of movement, and generally distracts you from your primary job.

---

[1]#DoItForShuby

My challenge to you is to scrutinize every day of your career, asking whether you're doing the best you can to add business value.

But what if your company incentivizes the wrong things? What if engineers can't get rewarded for doing what really helps the company but are instead rewarded for writing nice proposals, building things from scratch that should be bought, and generally stirring the pot? I've heard many, many engineers complain about this—I've never seen it be quite as bad as they say, but it is a problem. Well, I can offer two equally unsatisfying answers.

First, I've always found that doing the right thing is, in the end, rewarded. You can cheerfully do what you think is best, and it just might work out fine.

Second, if you feel that your company is pathologically committed to rewarding bad behavior, you can leave.

Saying No Is Not Your Job

When I was a young kernel engineer, I fell under the delusion that my job was to say "no." People working on a certain well-known phone were trying to move fast and ship products, which required them to put code into my codebase; my reaction was to complain that I should be reviewing, to say they were moving too fast, to say that things needed to be considered more carefully, and generally to delay and obstruct. Why?! Why didn't I make it my job to help them move as fast as they could with the best quality they could?

Well, eventually I did, but first I needed to overcome The Platform Engineer's Folly[2]—a toxic meme common among people who own core technical components, which I had absorbed from brilliant, friendly, experienced, but occasionally obstructionist people around me.

I use the term "platform engineer" (see Chapter 6) here to mean someone responsible for the ongoing maintenance of highly technical component that teams shipping products depend on—someone responsible for a core library, a storage system, a central service, etc. These people bear the weight of stewardship. If they mess up, the impact can be terrible, and yet people come to them every day with crazy, short-sighted requests to make their own lives easier ("I want to connect directly to the database for performance, the API is too slow"[3]). A large part of their job can become sifting through those requests to see which are crazy and which are sensible—every request is urgent, and other people don't feel the pain of maintenance.

---

[2] I just made that term up.
[3] This is a terrible idea; please do not do it.

And so, they often have to say "no"—most of the time, 100% correctly. And so, understandably, but incorrectly, they can come to feel that their customer base of product builders is always off the rails and that their job is to stop those people from messing up the platform. This is, however, false—their job is to enable those people.

I didn't develop that bad attitude based on hard experience of my own—I imitated it, secondhand, from experienced people who really had borne that burden of maintenance. So, my obstructionism was much more foolish—I simply thought that it literally was my job to always say, "I don't think we've thought this through enough," to find a reason to obstruct every feature request. For me, that meant missing several chances to be a part of something big in favor of trying to slow it down.

I'm relieved to say that I eventually fixed my malfunction and got to be the gas rather than the brakes; I hope you avoid that trap from the beginning. You will have to say "no," but less than always, and when you do, you should always try to come with an alternative suggestion of how your colleagues can get their jobs done.

Personal Reliability

We've just discussed how to act toward colleagues to build personal connections and mutual respect. In this section, we'll discuss another important ingredient to your reputation: reliability, the subjective sense that you can be trusted as a partner. This quality is prized almost as much brilliance in tech companies, for the simple reason that having partners let you down sucks and having partners come through for your rocks.

The most important ingredient to the confidence of peers and leaders is good execution—building good software speaks, to a certain extent, for itself. The rest of this book offers techniques for improving your execution, but here, we'll focus on how the *way* you do things affects trust.

Below, I'll list several practices I consider essential to signaling (and indeed, achieving) reliability. The theme running through these points is discipline—showing that we can control our impulses, focus, and apply ourselves for the good of the team.

Doing what we say: I trust it resonates that following through on what you say is the essence of reliability, whether it's sending an email, showing up to a meeting, fixing a bug, or even reviewing a tiny diff. One corollary to this is that when we lapse—which we all do, all the time—we should show that we take that failure seriously with an honest apology. A second is the importance of conservative estimation. I'll indulge in the cliché: it is indeed better to underpromise and overdeliver than vice versa.

Punctuality: I believe in punctuality. I believe showing up to meetings on time shows that you value your peers' time and creates a culture of vigorous execution, where strolling in five minutes late says that you don't really care if things happen exactly as they should. Be on time, every time. When you can't, your apology should be heartfelt—not "I forgot to put my laundry in the dryer" (a real example from an intern) but "I'm really sorry I'm late, folks, I got stuck in a tunnel."

Being available: We need our peers to get our work done. We need them to answer questions, review changes, fix problems in their code, and a million other things. When we can find them and get help instantly, we feel empowered and effective; when we have to wait, we feel a nauseous twinge of futility. Therefore, we trust people more when we can reach them during business hours. It's a luxury of our craft that we can usually come in late or pop out for errands if we need to; both look bad and are bad if done regularly. Replying to chats promptly can be annoying; just do it. Your colleagues will notice and appreciate if you're responsive, and they'll pull out their hair if they can't get a hold of you when they need to.

Running toward problems: When things are broken, I try to fix them— tests, scripts, dashboards, alerts, outages, and production code. Of course, this must be weighed against the urgency of our other tasks, but peers and leaders both notice who leans in for the benefit of all and who sits back to let someone else eventually come along and fix things.

Resisting distraction: You can't be focused every second of every day; breaks for coffee, chitchat, personal calls, and a little web browsing are an accepted part of programmer life. However, it's bad for your soul and your reputation if you spend a lot of time either slacking off or doing work not motivated by business value; don't let your colleague find that you're usually checking your stocks instead of your code when they walk by.

Businesslike language and body language: Sitting up reasonably straight, looking people in the eye, facing the speaker in a meeting, and avoiding profanity all contribute to the impression that you're engaged and here to work, not play. Of course, all of these practices are frequently relaxed in engineering environments—we literally put up our feet from time to time— but you should strive to practice these, especially around senior leaders.

Knowing Our Limits: The Epistemology of Software Engineering

Epistemology is the branch of philosophy concerned with the nature of knowledge—what it means to know something and how we can reason about what we and others know. It's a fascinating Wikipedia page and well worth a half hour's reading; there are many interesting thought experiments that challenge our intuitions about the nature of knowledge. I'm no philosopher, but I suspect that few of my readers will be either, so I'll try to get away with a minimally garbled example here.

Suppose you see a software engineer resembling your faithful author put a Pusheen the Cat plush toy into his pocket. Shortly after, we meet in person, and I ask you what is in my pocket. You confidently say that it's a Pusheen plush toy—and indeed it is. I'm fond of that Internet cat. However, the person you saw put the toy into his pocket was in fact my twin brother. So, did you know what was in my pocket? Your belief was true—I had a Pusheen toy in my pocket. It was justified—you saw someone who looked just like me put a toy into his pocket. But it wasn't me—so did you "know"?

In my opinion, a robust theory and caution about the boundaries of one's own knowledge are an important ingredient to trust with colleagues, and it typifies the best engineers—especially the best debuggers—I've known. They grasp what they well and truly know, what they believe, what they have good reason to suspect, and what they well and truly do not know. When problem-solving, that means that they can economically figure out what new knowledge would advance their understanding of a problem; when collaborating, it means that they seldom embarrass themselves with false assertions.

I hate to break it to you, but as a group, we're bad at this even in our own domain and doubly so when we speculate about all the other domains about which we know nothing. My advice to you is that when you're designing, coding, debugging, operating, or doing literally anything else in the universe of software endeavor, try to carefully catalog for yourself and others the level of confidence in your statements:

- **What you have directly observed**: Photons that have entered your very eyes, things you have extremely high confidence about (with allowance for the fact that that world can fool you!). For example, *I saw an error message in the logs saying, "Unable to connect to database: connection refused." It's a pretty good bet that you really saw that message, though it could mean many things.*

- **What you believe**: Things that you hold to be true about the world, substantiated by a credible chain of reasoning, but may not have personally directly verified beyond a shadow of a doubt. For example, *I believe this service talks to the database over an HAProxy load balancer, which was true the last time I looked at the code, though I haven't looked in a few months.*

- **What you suspect**: Things that may be true, supported by observation and belief. For example, *I looked at the database metrics, and I don't see any incoming requests on <this dashboard link>, so I'm suspecting that we may be having a problem with the HAProxy upgrade that's been going on this week.*

Navigating the differences between these tiers of knowledge can save you and your collaborators from many a red herring and save you a lot of face. If you lead with an observation rather than a conclusion, you let experts spot the real explanation that an incorrect inference would obscure; and a colleague who says things that are *true* is a trusted colleague.

Leading Others

If you deliver as an engineer, you'll eventually be asked to lead. That might mean driving a large project, mentoring your peers, or "tech leading" a team or subteam; it's work that goes beyond the technology you build and into how you guide the organization and individuals around you. Leadership requires humility and selflessness, compared to coding; as an engineer, you might be the action hero in your own little hacking movie, but as a leader, your job is to make the most of others' talents—to inspire them, to arm them with the context to make their own decisions, to keep them happy, and to help them improve on their weaknesses.

This section will offer tips for all of those enterprises; the one thing it won't discuss in detail is engineering management, though these practices apply to that job. "The Transition to Management" (Chapter 4) discusses how you can reason about that career move, but it's a subject well-treated in many other books.

Technical leadership has, above anything else, five dimensions. We'll list them here and then go into more detail.

- **Vision**: Choosing valuable, feasible things to do and crafting an inspiring story about those goals. That story isn't exactly the same as *what* you want to achieve; it's a narrative that links that work to a bigger picture and helps people take pride in their piece of the whole.

- **QA**: Making sure the team's code and practices are high quality.

© Daniel Heller 2020

D. Heller, *Building a Career in Software*, https://doi.org/10.1007/978-1-4842-6147-7_8

- **Project management**: Planning, tracking, and communication to divide work into coherent pieces, allocate the right resources, do the right things at the right times, and remember the loose ends.

- **Harmony**: Fostering a collaborative environment where team members respect each other but also feel safe and valued as individuals.

- **Mentorship**: Shepherding the growth of your team members as individuals, including teaching, feedback, and career advice.

After that, we'll discuss a couple of common specific scenarios: onboarding engineers to a team and managing an intern.

Vision and Identity

In my experience, engineers are driven above all by the desire to do work that matters, and when they feel that they're contributing to something wonderful, other ills will be overcome, ignored, or forgiven; when people don't buy the vision or feel an identity as a team, then no amount of nurture, fun, or money will keep them happy. Therefore, I think a strong vision is the most important part of a leader's work, whether on a project, a team, or a whole organization. A tech lead may only control part of that vision (engineering managers or product managers will own part of it), but there's usually room for maneuver—maybe you can add a project that matters, maybe you can cancel one that isn't feasible, or maybe you can articulate the narrative that will inspire people to execute on the plan.

When you have the leeway to make your own roadmap, far and away your foremost tool is research (see "Having Your Own Project Ideas" in Chapter 3). Read, ask people (your team members, your peers, your customers, your manager) their opinions, estimate impact, estimate cost, and tell the story that you're doing the project with the biggest bang for your team's buck.

However you source your plan, engineers need to feel proud to be part of it, which means you need to tell them a story that makes them proud. I've seen a few successful templates; each of them tells the team members something about themselves to take pride in. Try one, or come up with your own:

- This is an opportunity that can change the company (or the world). If you deliver, the upside will be huge.

Our goal is to drive the load time of the site from 1.5s at p95 to 750ms. This is a hard problem, but our team has the expertise, and if we do it, we can bring in over $50 million next year in improved conversion rates.

- This is an existential threat, and your team are the saviors. If the team doesn't deliver, it may be disaster, even the end of the company.

At the rate the business is scaling, our main database is going to fall over in six months. This migration is going to be painful, but if we don't do it, the company will not survive; we're going to make scaling problems a thing of the past.

- This is the smartest, most careful team, the stewards whose expertise and diligence put everyone else on track.

We are the stewards of production at this company. This is a tough and sometimes thankless job, but our diligence saves hours of downtime and millions of dollars.

- This is the team that gets things done. Maybe others are more technical, but this team ships code that matters while others dither.

Our company's business is driven by integrating smoothly with every customer installation. Today, we cover 85%, and our sales engineers sweat to cover the difference. Our goal is to bridge this gap, save tons of money on sales engineering, and unlock another order of magnitude of scaling.

As you can see, some of these involve a certain element of opposition, drawing a contrast between your team and the rest of the world; a touch of "us versus them" is a helpful device as long as it doesn't go so far as to breed outrage or hostility.

Team QA

As a technical leader, part of your job is making sure your software and practices are high quality. I basically believe in three methods for achieving this: leading by example, direct feedback, and teaching your principles.

Leading by example should speak for itself—if the engineers you lead see you ship crappy code or play fast and loose with production, they'll learn to do the same. If they see you hold yourself to a shockingly high standard, they'll absorb that too. This method shouldn't be underestimated; I find that young engineers are hungry for inspiration, and when they recognize admirable practices, they'll strive to emulate them.

Second, you can give 1:1 feedback (a subject unto itself); this is an opportunity for more nuance and detail. Code review and design review are a tech lead's most frequent opportunities to share and enforce their standards.

Finally, sharing your principles in writing and in presentations is the most scalable way to evangelize your practices; a presentation on operational practices can reach a whole team in one-tenth the time of giving direct feedback to everyone. I favor one-page white papers, runbooks, and slide decks especially—each give you opportunities to crisply codify your standards. I think every team should have at a minimum a document that captures its deployment and on-call practices, but you might get good mileage out of a style guide, a position paper on reliability practice, etc., etc.

Project Management

Project management as a leader is, more or less, a scaling up of project managing yourself (Chapter 5). I'll only mention two extensions to those principles.

Communication

When you lead a project, you depend on the discretion and creativity of your team members. In order for them to make good decisions and have good ideas, they need to know what's going on, not just to the minimum necessary to execute on tasks but in the big picture; that context lets them connect their work to others' and find mutual opportunities (or common problems). You should strive to avoid making yourself the only conduit of information. This is an important argument for a weekly team meeting where everyone discusses what they've done in the past week. That meeting isn't for you as the leader, though you might benefit—you could certainly get the whole picture from 1:1s. Its foremost purpose is to cross-pollinate across engineers.

It also colors how you assign tasks. If you tell an engineer, "we are migrating from Memcached to Redis for these data; please move all the call sites onto the Redis client," they really don't know what's going on; that's confusing and, to a knowledgeable professional, insulting. Moreover, they then depend exclusively on you for more information, which is inefficient for both of you. I've had countless tasks assigned to me with exactly that much context, and it's always driven me nuts. In contrast, if you explain the motivation in detail and provide links for further information, you arm a professional to make their own way. In contrast to the above:

When we built this system, there was no common caching framework; we used Memcached because Tina was very familiar with it. Now, all the teams are aligning on Redis, which is going to have much better operational support, so we need to migrate off of Memcached. Ashish on that team is our point of contact.

Assigning Work

The second extension is about the subtle art of assigning tasks to the right owners. Whole books are written on this topic, and I won't aspire to a complete treatment. I'll just offer one tip: the ideal task for a given engineer is "what they've shown they can do, plus epsilon"—the ideal work is always a chance for them to grow, for the good of the team and for their own satisfaction, but not a wild shot in the dark that will require constant hand-holding. And, given that the ideal task always pushes an engineer, we should acknowledge that upfront and repeatedly check in on how they're doing, offering help if they need it—if we don't offer, junior people will usually think they aren't welcome to ask.

Harmony

As a lead, you're the shepherd not just of projects but of people, and you can contribute to your team's execution by creating a harmonious atmosphere. Since many books have been written on this subject, I'll offer only my top two suggestions.

First, always set a tone of positivity and optimism. A group of people will naturally key off the emotional tone of their leader, and when you're pessimistic or angry, they will be too. Giving credit liberally and publicly and celebrating what goes right can create an atmosphere of positivity. Deriding or insulting your team does quite the opposite and should be avoided at all costs; your criticism hits twice as hard as anyone else's. You'll experience frustration, pessimism, and anger, but venting them is not the luxury of a leader (which is one of the great challenges of leadership); find your calm and positivity every day.

Second, keep an eye on people. If you sense that they're upset or stressed, you can go miles by just saying what you see and asking if you can help; just as your criticism hits hard, so can your empathy.

Mentorship

In software, we're asked to mentor from very early in our careers—onboarding colleagues, mentoring interns, and helping junior teammates as soon as we've learned enough to have something to teach. I've had several managers in my career, observed many more, and done my own share of management. In my experience, most of us, including me, pursue the enterprise of mentorship at best haphazardly; we seldom have a long-term plan, and we struggle to find opportunities to move the needle. In this section, I propose a more systematic playbook for mentorship. I'll discuss

- The goals of mentorship
- How to model the abilities and progress of your mentee
- Tools for teaching, evaluation, and getting the most out of 1:1s
- Integrating those tools in long-term plan

Your Purpose As a Mentor

Your goals as a mentor are to help your mentee become a better engineer or manager, contribute to the success of your company, and achieve their own goals. I posit five core components of that work:

1. **Teaching**: Sharing practices and insights from your greater experience, putting new tools in your mentee's toolbox.

2. **Support and comfort**: The support of a mentor, particularly one who *isn't* also a manager responsible for performance reviews, can be a great relief in stressful times.

3. **Evaluation**: Assessing strengths and weaknesses, figuring out where to focus mentoring efforts.

4. **Tactical problem-solving**: Helping your mentee navigate specific situations that arise in their day-to-day work.

5. **Goal setting**: Helping clarify actionable, valuable goals; note that even experienced people may grapple with where to go next in their careers.

All of the above are challenging; it takes good listening, emotional intelligence, and creativity to adapt your methods to an individual with their own communication style, desires, and abilities. Those challenges, and your guaranteed fallibility as a mentor, lead to two critical ancillary goals:

A. **Building trust**: Creating the shared context, openness, and supportive environment that will allow for candor.

B. **Listening and learning**: Taking feedback from your mentee, figuring out where you're going wrong and how you can do better.

A Model of Your Mentee

Your model of your mentee—an idea of what they want and where they stand—determines how you'll approach your task. I argue that you should have such a model in mind at all times in order to always reason clearly about your priorities as a mentor.

Goals

Some mentees have strong and specific desires—mastering a specific technology, getting a promotion, becoming a manager, executing a transition to product management, etc., etc., etc. These are the easy ones; most likely, when you hear their goal, you can help them craft a plan.

Most engineers, though, are much more vague in their aspirations; they more or less just know they want to Get Better. You should help them clarify their thinking if you can, but I also argue: some vagueness is fine. In the absence of specific goals, there's one direction for an engineer, which is up and to the right: bigger impact, more complex problems, more autonomy, better quality, better communication, better project management, and so on. By default, we can set a goal of a new standard of excellence for ourselves, pick a small number of points to focus on, and start on the work.

I recommend discussing goals in depth with a mentee in your first few meetings, then no less than quarterly as you continue to work together; set yourself a calendar reminder.

A Vector of Skills

Success in engineering or management requires a portfolio of complementary skills; success in mentorship requires a model of your mentee's skills relative to their goals. I recommend keeping in mind this vector of competencies and regularly asking yourself—and your mentee—where they stand; that clarity will help you allocate your time.

I believe that evaluating performance is a hard or impossible problem which can only be approached patiently, with great attention over time, if at all. Subsequent sections will suggest exercises intended to both benefit your mentee and inform you, but the process in any case begins with an idea of what you want to evaluate. Here's where I start:

1. **Coding**: Clarity, testing, documentation, and discipline in scope of differences

2. **Project management**: Identifying dependencies, updating stakeholders, and tracking tasks

3. **Communication**: Clear emails and engaging presentations

4. **Personal organization and time management**: Not dropping balls but prioritizing effectively

5. **Architecture**: The macroscopic design of systems

6. **Leadership/mentorship**: At a level appropriate to their position

7. **Emotional skills**: Confidence, stress management, and work–life balance

Tools for Getting Organized

I conceive mentoring as centered around 1:1 meetings happening every 1–2 weeks for 30–60 minutes. In this section, I'll offer a menu of tools for teaching and evaluation in 1:1s; a later section will propose a scheme for integrating these pieces in a longer-term strategy.

Since your goal is complex and there are many tools available, deciding how to spend your time is instantly challenging. Luckily, you don't need every moment to fit perfectly into a grand scheme. Stay organized with a shared doc, try to align on goals, and ask good questions—then you can be intuitive and flexible as you build your sense of your mentee and come up with a plan.

I only have one recommendation I consider mandatory: be proactive. Asking a report, "how's it going," is no crime—but when that doesn't lead to deep insight, as it often won't, you should have tools for getting somewhere interesting.

Agenda Doc

Frequency: Every meeting

Don't be stateless! Keep an agenda doc you can both update where you record topics for your meetings; also stash key takeaways there. As you explore different ways of working together, your shared doc will help you stay organized and avoid getting overwhelmed. Keep your own private notes too, where you record areas to follow up on. Closing open loops helps you get the most out of your discussions, and being organized shows your commitment to your mentee.

Goal Setting

Frequency: Once per quarter

The main purpose of goal setting is to help your mentee clarify their thinking about long-term plans, but that process also helps you deepen your understanding of your mentee and do your own planning. Adapt your approach to the maturity and level of certainty of your mentee, whether that means brainstorming ideas together or diving in on the gritty details. Set yourself a calendar reminder to have this discussion quarterly, and be sure to record the results in your shared document.

Tools for Getting the Most from 1:1s

The Top Two Problems

Frequency: Every meeting

In some 1:1s, particularly as you're getting to know each other, you'll likely find it hard to get the conversation going; even if there's plenty going on, it can be hard to decide what to talk about. I suggest asking your mentee to come to your meetings ready to discuss the two most pressing problems they're facing. Those problems might be from any domain—technology, interpersonal issues, organizational issues, project management, etc., etc. This method is easy, it offers opportunities to advise on important issues, and you'll find that you often segue to other interesting topics.

Probing Questions

Frequency: Once per month or whenever you have time

It's good to leave space in your 1:1s for unstructured conversation—it's a refreshing change of pace and an opportunity to hear things from your mentee you might not in a more focused conversation. I've often found that people have plenty to say but need prompting: where "how's it going" or "what's on your mind" might stall, a more specific question can get people talking. Have a few off-the-shelf questions ready to go. It can feel stilted, but stomach it, and be candid about the fact that it's a way to start the conversation; once the discussion gets going, ask good follow-up questions! Learn something about how your mentee sees things.

Upward Feedback

Frequency: Once per quarter, if not more

Your mentoring is imperfect, in general and in each case in particular; feedback from your mentee helps you improve. At least once a quarter, you should solicit feedback about what's been useful (or the opposite) in your mentoring. It may or may not go without saying that you should genuinely appreciate it when a mentee has the guts to give you honest feedback about how you can improve. This is also a good time to ask yourself, and maybe your mentee, the question: Is this interaction still valuable? The day can come when interests, needs, or circumstances change, and a mentorship relationship can come to an end.

Chitchat

Frequency: Every meeting

Ask about the long weekend; ask about the most recent episode of their favorite show; ask about their vacation. And in turn, talk about your long weekend, share what you thought about GoT, and tell them about your trip to the Computer History Museum. Taking a genuine interest in your mentee and sharing of yourself are important ways to build trust, and they can help you find enjoyment in the work of mentorship. A 1:1 dominated by chit chat doesn't serve its purpose, but take some time to enjoy a conversation.

Answer with a Question

Suggesting that you reply to questions with "what do you think?" is more or less a cliché—but it can give your mentee a chance to formulate their own ideas, and it's a confidence boost when they're onto something. Give it a try.

Tools for Deep Dives

As you develop a sense of your mentee's goals and abilities, you'll identify areas where you want to focus your teaching. This section will suggest a few ways you can go deeper in a specific area.

Exercises

Frequency: As needed

Exercises in a given area can take the form of reviewing recent work, simulating a task, or producing a real product—the goal is to practice a skill, provide signal to both parties about progress, and give the mentor an opportunity to give meaningful feedback.

For example:

- Review recent emails together to improve communication.

- Review recent diffs together to improve code clarity.

- Write a hypothetical roadmap for a team as a management exercise.

- Choose a task tracking app, and use it for two weeks to improve organization.

- Make a list of potential new roles to review together when considering a change.

Book Club

Frequency: As needed

You probably have a book, article, blog post, or paper in mind for any focus area you might tackle with your mentee. I've found it productive to have a "book club" together—suggest some reading material, then discuss

- Key insights
- Weaknesses
- Relevance to current work

It can add some nice variety and encourage your mentee to develop their own practice of educational reading.

Reviews and Postmortems

Frequency: once per month

You're both constantly finishing projects, coming from meetings, interviewing candidates, etc., etc., etc.; discuss some of those events. Include

- What went right
- What went wrong
- What you'd do differently

As always, look for the general principle at work that your mentee can file away.

Putting the Pieces Together

We now have all too many building blocks for mentorship—the part I've consistently found hardest is integrating these pieces in a coherent way. I suggest a few key elements to help you balance long-term strategy with improvisation:

1. **Goal setting once per quarter**: Set a calendar reminder!

2. **Subject matter "units"** focused in service of those goals—for instance, three 1:1s in a row focused on project management, with exercises and reading. You should aim to identify such a theme at least once a quarter.

3. **A default of discussing tactical issues** if no broader units occur to either of you; look for broader lessons in those issues. These ad hoc conversations can offer a casual break from focused sessions. Fall back on "two top issues" and off-the-shelf questions.

4. **A liberal attitude toward diversions that arise along the way**: Enjoy them, and learn from them together when they occur.

5. **Transparency about your process** and collaboration with your mentee on making your plans; you should encourage them to take as active a role as possible in planning and discussion.

6. **Time thinking about your mentee on your own**: Don't only consider your mentee when they're in front of your face. I suggest scheduling a dedicated half hour per month, the output of which should be a refined assessment of their skills and several proposals for subjects to cover together.

7. **Regular replanning**: You may only set goals once a quarter, and you may sometimes spend several sessions in deep discussion of tactical questions. But, when you reach the end of the tunnel, step back, and think a bit about the future. Bring a list of ideas to your meeting, and discuss together: What's something we could go deep on in the next month?

Onboarding Engineers

Regardless of whether you lead groups, you'll likely sometimes take charge of onboarding new people to your team. I once saw this done well, but I may have dreamt it—it's usually done terribly. I vividly remember simply having no one tell me anything when I started one job; I just got a task and got to work.

As we've discussed in Chapter 4, joining a new team is a bewildering experience even for seasoned engineers, but if you're in charge of onboarding someone, you can save them some suffering. Here's what I recommend.

Before your new arrival joins, prep a one-page document for them. This should include links to key wikis and dashboards or a list of owners for key areas they may need to work in.

Once they join, immediately kick off your collaboration with a one-hour onboarding meeting. In that meeting, you should cover the following:

- The team's mission
- An overview of the team's architecture on a white board, with pictures taken at the end for posterity
- A discussion of the major projects going on in the team
- A discussion of any key principles, values, or practices on the team and any special gotchas
- A review of your larger organization, including an overview of the key engineers and managers in the organization and their portfolios
- A Q&A

Finally, you should make it your business to be obnoxiously available for questions; this should be proactive, because new hires are shy and scared to ask. I suggest checking in at the beginning and end of every single day, asking how their work is going and if they need anything.

After your own first onboarding, which will probably be haphazard at best, you'll probably be completely sold on this mindful approach.

Interns

Within a couple of years of starting your career, you're likely to manage an intern. Cool! If you've read the above sections, you're ready to lead and mentor just about anyone; I'll just add practical details specific to interns.

Most internships are structured around one project. An intern is assigned an "Intern Manager," who is usually a fairly junior engineer; the collaboration is seen as an opportunity for both parties, with the intern manager getting a chance to practice leadership. The team manager and the intern manager will agree together on a project, which is almost always far away from the team's critical path (if an intern is on the critical path, the team is in for some trouble).

The most important things to remember about interns are

- They don't know anything.
- They aren't going to tell you when they're off track.

Therefore, proactive mentoring and monitoring are the key to managing interns. Like most management, you should have a weekly 30-minute 1:1 where you review project status and where questions are welcome. As with all new employees, you should check in frequently to confirm that all is well—initially daily, later a couple of times per week. You should plan to go deep on your intern's questions, not just telling them what command to run but delving into the theory of the team's technology and methods. Perhaps most importantly, to keep them on track, you should set the project schedule, including deadlines for numerous milestones, like an early design review, a full design review, a prototype review, and projected completion. When managing a seasoned professional, managers will often ask the engineer to set deadlines, because they know best. With an intern, however, deadlines keep things on track, especially because they create frequent opportunities for the mentor to review the intern's work; this avoids the (common) intern worst case, which is letting a false start fester for weeks before anyone notices.

Adversity

In Which: Things Go Wrong

This chapter is a guide to some of the bad things that happen in software: stress, conflict, and breaking the build. I'll offer a perspective on a selection of problems that I've found particularly taxing in my own career and that I've seen others struggle with. The theme running through them all won't surprise you: bad things happen all the time, but they're never a reason to lapse in your professionalism.

Managing Your Emotions

Engineering will challenge your self-control.

I've seen a Staff Engineer throw a tantrum in a huge meeting, berating another team for their politics; I've seen a colleague burst into tears and flee a room during a discussion of some problems their team was having; I personally have more than once told off a colleague when I perceived condescension, and in college, I once went to the hospital after a template-related C++ error led me to punch a metal doorframe (it really was a tiny tap, I don't know what happened).

I find each of these outbursts completely relatable, even with the benefit of years of mellowing. The staff engineer was under tremendous pressure; the fleeing colleague had tried extremely hard to fix those team problems and felt overwhelmed; and those times I told off a colleague were in the greatest

© Daniel Heller 2020

D. Heller, *Building a Career in Software*, https://doi.org/10.1007/978-1-4842-6147-7_9

period of professional stress of my entire life. I've usually dug up some sympathy in my heart for colleagues who occasionally vent their stress or frustration under pressure.

Nevertheless, this isn't what we want—emotional eruptions fray the harmony of a team, and they're apt to challenge the confidence and enthusiasm of even supportive colleagues. I think that resilience and magnanimity are two of the defining traits of true professionals and cultivating them is essential on the journey to professionalism. Your goal should be to always maintain calm and civility in group settings, even when under pressure, even when condescended to.

But how, in the face of deadlines, sleep deprivation, and snark?

Well, resilience is more art than science—unfortunately, this section is more call to action than it is a manual, and I don't know what'll work for you. But I'll tell you what works, most of the time, for me:

- **To prepare for recognizing and managing my emotions**: Meditation, 5–10 minutes a day. Ten seconds of googling will find you countless guided meditations you can try, but I personally just sit, breathe, and try to let my mind empty.

- **To stay cool in moments of strain**: A deep breath and a careful analysis of my body, recognizing that I'm stressed or angry and trying to let it go.

- **To find my empathy**: Reflecting on how others' misbehavior probably comes from their own struggle and doing my best to find empathy for them.

- **To blow off steam**: Pop out for a coffee or a walk, pet a dog, or do a small amount of complaining to a trusted friend or colleague.

Good luck, my friend!

Yes, Things Are Broken (You Can't Fix Everything on Your First Day)

When you join a new company or team, it's very possible that you'll discover things you hate about their practices or quality: they put the braces on their own line; they use Jira instead of Phabricator (or vice versa); they use Gerrit instead of GitHub; they use Maven instead of Gradle; they don't have nearly enough test coverage. When that happens, don't let yourself become overwhelmed with outrage; resist the pull to start telling everyone how wrong they are about everything.

You may be right about everything, though you're more likely missing context or just intoxicated by a strong preference. Which it is doesn't matter—you aren't going to get everyone to change everything (or maybe, anything) before you've earned your team's trust, and you won't get far by insulting the decisions you didn't have the hard job of making. Start by listening: ask why things are done a certain way, and ask with an open mind. Continue by contributing: build some social capital (i.e., trust and goodwill) by doing things the team needs. Then, in good time, pick one thing you want to change, and try to change it not by acting like the current choice is dumb but by making a positive, humble case for the advantages of change.

Conflict Resolution and Dealing with Difficult People

Kindness: Plans A, B, and C

Compared to when I started in the industry (2007), our collective tolerance for bad behavior of every type has radically shrunk; the way old hands at my first job talked to me would be almost unthinkable today. Still, we engineers aren't known for our diplomacy, and you're likely to encounter infuriating people at work—people who talk down to you, reject your diffs with pedantic trivialities, make rude comments in meetings, etc.

The recipe for dealing with them is simple: warmth, kindness, and assertiveness are the solution 98% of the time—defuse and stay on topic. The foremost reason for that is that it's the right thing to do; I'd rather walk through my day with grace than anger, and I'm sure you would too. The second reason, more to the point, is that calm and kindness get far and away better results. Here's why:

1. Many times, someone who's rude is experiencing some distress of their own. Speaking to them with kindness, even asking if they're stressed out, can help them and turn a potential adversary into an ally.

2. People who are actually wrongheaded (as opposed to just having a bad day/week) are still apt to warm to kindness; again, you should take your shot at making a friend rather than an enemy.

3. Even if kindness doesn't get good results in the moment, hostility can't easily be undone; it's usually better to let bad behavior slide than escalate to real conflict.

4. How you deal with difficult people plays into your broader reputation; a reputation for patience and kindness will pay you back in a whole organization's eagerness to work with you and, more often than you'd think, in positive feedback to your boss that pays off at performance review time.

Responding to jerkishness with kindness is tough. When someone talks down to me at work, I feel a surge of simian aggression, a heart rate spike and an urge toward physical violence, or at least to deliver a burn clever enough to require hospitalization—responding productively takes discipline. I'm pleased to say that I've seldom responded with hostility and never come close to criminal battery.

Graciousness is, however, fully compatible with assertiveness—you can swallow your savage comebacks while staying on topic and on message, and that poise will often impress others. Keeping your cool now also doesn't rule out a stronger response in the future. You'll need your own strategy, but here are two solid techniques to start with.

If in person: Take a very deep breath, and let it out slowly (really), and I think, "you [meaning yourself] are going to regret this." I know the latter is true because 99% of the times I've responded to someone with anger, I've regretted it.[1]

If by email: Never, ever send an email in anger. If my blood is boiling while writing an email, I always let it cool down as a draft for at least a few hours, and usually overnight. Angry emails are disasters for professional relationships—they're durable, easy to forward, and people tend to reread and stew on them. I've written quite a lot of angry emails, but after letting them ripen overnight, I almost always succeed in clicking "Delete" instead of "Send."

Here are a few tactics you can try when a conversation turns tense.

In a Meeting or by Email

It sounds like you're especially concerned about X for reason Y; that makes sense to me. I'll take the action item to discuss this with you after offline. We'll make sure {it's handled/we find a good compromise/we weigh the tradeoffs carefully}.

---

[1] If anyone reading this remembers an incident of my telling someone they were about to get some "straight talk" in a meeting, I'm sorry; it was a bad week.

Here, you acknowledge the legitimacy of another point of view without giving in and defer continued discussion until you both have a chance to cool off. Both of these increase the likelihood that you can find common ground when you resume.

It seems we may prioritize A vs B differently. I think that favoring B is very justifiable. I'll try to explain why I favor A.

Here, you explicitly identify a point of disagreement, acknowledge the legitimacy of your counterpart's reasoning, and immediately segue into your argument. Your genial acknowledgement of a well-intentioned difference of opinion defuses the tension and attempts to turn an emotional situation into a shared analysis.

One on One

Is everything okay? You seem like you might be a little stressed out.

This question isn't for every day, but if you think someone really is on edge, a show of human concern can build a lasting bridge. A great professional friendship of mine once began when a colleague acted out in a meeting; I keyed up to berate him, but then calmed myself and asked this question. It turned out that he was indeed stressed out; we talked about it, and we got along forever after.

I got the sense you were frustrated with how that meeting went. I definitely get that it's a tough issue. Can we chat about how to address those concerns?

Similarly, you try to transition a tense public conversation into a friendly 1:1 discussion where your counterpart feels heard.

A *related* indirect option: grab a coffee together after the meeting and don't even talk about the issue, just try to get to know each other a little better.

Plan D

There are a few other tools in the toolbox:

- **Manager feedback**: If you've tried to build a good collaboration with someone repeatedly and failed, you can go over their head and give feedback to a manager. If this becomes necessary, again, you should be slow to escalate, because the toothpaste doesn't go back in the tube. Remember that managers may have their own frustrations with their teams, but the team is an extension of the manager herself; you should be as gentle as you would be giving feedback to someone about themselves. Balancing your criticism with praise shows that you want a friendly interaction. You can try out: "Rick has done <thing X> really well, and we've appreciated his help, but we've gotten a bit stuck on <thing Y>—can you help us make sure it's prioritized?" On the other hand, if someone is causing *big* problems—outages, emotional distress to colleagues, etc.—you may have to be direct.

- **HR**: For certain classes of misbehavior—harassment, bullying, lawbreaking—your company's human resources department may be the right escalation path. As discussed in "Dealing with HR," you should remember that HR is the company's representative, not yours, but at least at US companies, it's usually the designated path raising issues of mistreatment.

- **(Very, very rarely.) Anger**: once in a great while, responding with a small amount of hostility can be beneficial—very occasionally, someone needs to find out that you're not going to put up with their behavior. I'd consider this an absolute last resort when you've already tried kindness repeatedly and failed and manager feedback either fails or isn't an option. If you have to use it (or can't help yourself), I strongly advise you to follow-up by apologizing and trying to build a bridge. Remember, though—it's 100x easier to keep it together the first time than to rebuild a relationship.

Dealing with HR

Human Resources (HR) departments operate the machinery of employment—hiring, firing, and trying to maximize the value companies get from their employees. In the United States, HR is also typically responsible for compliance with employment regulations—it helps the firm avoid embarrassment and liability by ensuring that the company complies with the law as it relates to employees. That means that HR is, in many companies, the venue for complaints about harassment or discrimination; it protects the company's interests by preventing illegal mistreatment of employees. Notably, reports of discriminatory activity have some protection from retaliation in the United States.[2]

HR is, first and last, a representative of your employer. That means that it may well help you but that it represents your employer's interests, rather than yours. In the following, I'll share two day-to-day suggestions from my own experience, but if you have a real HR problem, you may want to consult an expert who does have a duty to your interests, like a lawyer.

In my experiences with both good and bad HR departments, two practices have served me well. First, I am ceaselessly my own advocate—I don't assume that HR has done anything for me unless I see an explicit confirmation it's happened. Lapsing on this one once left me stranded for a month without a visa! And second, when dealing with HR, including recruiters, HR Business Partners, compensation discussions, etc., etc., etc., I keep detailed records in my personal email, which has timestamps and which I fully control. I've more than once been glad I could refer to a record of exactly what was said and when.

Making Mistakes

For my part, I've made some pretty nasty ones, sweated and loathed myself, and more or less made my peace with them. I once wrote 20 synchronization primitives in assembly but left a single barrier instruction out of a single one; it made us think we had a processor bug, and 10 highly paid people did nothing but debug for 2 weeks. A few years later, a cascading failure in a system my team owned brought down several product features for 90 nauseating minutes, an extravagantly expensive black eye. In each case, I owned my mistakes and wasn't even censured with a single word, less still fired.

As I once said to a brilliant colleague who was dejected after causing an outage: it's easy to avoid outages if you never do anything. Good engineers push themselves, and they seldom work on perfect systems with perfect unit and integration testing; mistakes are inevitable, and some of them are going

---

[2]*www.eeoc.gov/retaliation*

to have consequences. As long as you mean well and truly strive to responsibly follow best practices, that's basically fine. I've only once seen an engineer fired for a technical mistake (a really bad one) and only twice seen an engineer suffer career consequences for single mistakes.

There are only two things to remember. First, be completely forthright; hiding a mistake shows that you're untrustworthy, which is much worse than causing a bug. In fact, I've always found that my colleagues have respected it when people stand up and take responsibility for problems. Second, don't beat yourself up too much. Own your mistake, get a good night's sleep, remember that you're neither the first nor the last engineer to cause a problem, and move on.

Professional Conduct

In Which We Aspire to a Code (Not to Code)

Let's aspire to a sense of pride and honor in our work. No book has influenced my thinking about the craft of engineering more than Uncle Bob's *The Clean Coder*. He observes that lawyers and doctors are bound by a code of both ethics and strong professional standards that give others a reasonable confidence in their conduct and reliability. That's not to say that every doctor or lawyer is honorable or capable, but it does mean that as a field, they demand a great deal of themselves.

I found this an inspiring idea, but I didn't truly internalize it until I happened to have a conversation about work with a pediatric surgeon. Three things struck me: an iron determination to help her patients, a level of refinement in her training that I had never before observed firsthand, and the explicit idea that the opportunity to care for others is a great privilege. I was moved, and shaken; I wanted to hold myself to a standard that high and realized that I never had.

© Daniel Heller 2020
D. Heller, *Building a Career in Software*, https://doi.org/10.1007/978-1-4842-6147-7_10

We may not all help individuals like a surgeon, but we can all challenge ourselves to raise our standards; we can aim to be not just coders but craftspeople, practitioners of excellence and ethics. And so, I come to the question of professional conduct. Here's what I'd offer:

- **Treat your colleagues with respect**: First and foremost, respect your colleagues: your words and actions should help every single colleague feel included, justly treated, and comfortable enough to do their best work every single day. Doing so demands both individual respect and consideration of broader context—anti-racism, opposition to sexism, and general commitment to justice and inclusion.

- **Do your very best to follow through on what you say**: Give others a reason to trust your word without fail.

- **Nurture your skills as a point of pride**: Aim to be better than you have to be, continuously growing and improving.

Professionalism can feel thankless—other people are goofing off and being rude, so who cares if you do? My experience is that people appreciate it more than you'd think—when I've changed roles, people have often come up to me and thanked me for my professionalism. I have as many off days and slips of temper as you do, but if you get up every day and strive to show your colleagues consideration, appreciation, and respect, people notice. In the following sections, I'll help you avoid what I've found to be the most common professionalism pitfalls.

A Word About Complaining

Casual complaining is software engineers' favorite pastime. We read bad code, we argue with pointy-haired bosses and project managers, and we fight broken tools; sometimes, we just have to let it out.[1] Those frustrations are real, and sharing them can be an important release; as an industry, we also prize a playful cynicism that can make complaining seem like part of the game. I love a good kvetching session, and I'll grant that, properly channeled, shared complaints can be the start of something great—"this is crap, and by gosh we're going to make it better together." That said, I've officially retired from the sport of complaining at work, and I advise you to partake infrequently, because it's easy for complaining to poison a team's spirit. Please note, before

---

[1] Every job in the world is frustrating, software engineering perhaps less than most, but okay, frustration is the human condition.

I explain this problem, the critical distinction between casual grousing—blowing off steam about everyday frustrations—and the unrelated necessity of discussing serious problems like discrimination, which is always appropriate.

I have, and you will, encounter teams whose dialogue descends into tireless whining. Their grievances may be real, and yet, if they could see themselves, I think they would be embarrassed—having lunch or coffee without a word on any subject except insult to other (well-intentioned) teams and technology, evidently in a loop where each complaint encourages the next. This is the risk of grumbling: our catharsis can bring down the people around us, potentially low enough that no one has a good word left to say. When we sink to where we can never balance complaints with optimism, we should take it as a sign that it's time to fix our attitude or move on—find a way to be a part of building something positive.

A Word About Gossip

I've lived to regret every bad thing I've ever said about a colleague behind their back. I think I do it less than most (I certainly try to resist the urge), but I've lapsed from time to time. Ragging on a frustrating colleague can be spectacularly cathartic, a bonding experience with a like-minded friend, and generally a fun and relaxing time; and as far as I know it's never blown back on me—I can't deny it.

But we degrade ourselves and our team when we do it. A healthy team depends on mutual trust and support, on some generosity of spirit between teammates; insulting people behind their backs frays that fabric. Moreover, people admire grace and generosity and in the end look down on venom. When I left my first job and several people came up to me and told me that they'd appreciated my professionalism, I was amazed to realize that people noticed my efforts to be kind, and I felt a stab of shame for all my lapses in speaking ill of others. When shit-talking breaks out, I suggest you speak up in defense of the maligned whenever you can—if you can't, waiting out the conversation is far better than piling on.

A Word About Office Dating

I think office dating is a bad idea, and I advise you to avoid it.[2,3]

---

[2]I'll start with my confession: I have in fact twice dated colleagues. I once had a girlfriend I met at an internship, and I went on a single date with a colleague around ten years ago; I will never date a colleague again. Hopefully, the above won't distract you from the point.
[3]Several of my beloved friends met their partners at work; I don't hold it against them.

For anyone who didn't know before, #MeToo made it clear that we have a big, big problem with sexual harassment in the tech workplace. I argue: accept no risk of becoming part of the problem. Your colleague may indeed be interested in you but why risk making them uncomfortable, making it harder to work together, and possibly harming their and your career?

On top of the traditional options of friends and activities, OkCupid, Bumble, Grindr, Tinder, Coffee Meets Bagel, Hinge, Zoosk, and I don't know how many other dating apps are out there overflowing with people looking to date; our era probably enjoys more alternatives to workplace dating than any other in human history. In my opinion, this makes it even harder to justify the risk of distressing a coworker with an unwanted romantic advance. Bring your best professional conduct, and only your professional conduct, to the office, and you'll never have to wonder whether you did the right thing.

Choosing Our Words Carefully

I once heard an engineer scream an exceptionally vulgar obscenity, a reference to a TV show, at the top of his lungs at the office. Mortified, enraged, and panickedly looking over my own shoulder for colleagues I assumed to already be calling HR, I hissed at him that he was out of line; he replied that the office isn't a place where you have to behave in a special way. I couldn't disagree more if I tried; I was confident then, and am quite confident now, that the workplace demands extraordinary care with language.

This section will explore the necessity to choose our words to maximize the comfort of our colleagues. Other sources can illuminate important topics like workplace law, inclusion, and microaggression in detail, but I feel that I must touch on this subject, because I've observed that many engineers feel a misplaced liberty to use language at work that makes others uncomfortable.

First, some legal context. This discussion is specific to the United States, but similar rules may apply in other countries. In the United States, the law promises workers freedom from harassment in the workplace. Harassment is defined as "unwelcome conduct that is based on race, color, religion, sex (including pregnancy), national origin, age (40 or older), disability or genetic information."[4] A company is responsible for providing that safe environment and can be sued if it fails to; harassers may also be personally liable in some cases. Just as offense need not be intended to be given, you need not intend any harm for your behavior to distress others and meet the legal definition of harassment; this fact alone should give you pause.

Second, an ethical observation: we should hold our language not to the standard of what we think people should be comfortable with, but rather to

---

[4]www.eeoc.gov/harassment, fetched 2020-06-10.

the standard of allowing real comfort, of creating a workplace where everyone can do their best work in peace. It should go without saying that we never discomfit others intentionally, but even if you don't foresee how your words hurt others, or if feel that you should be able to use term X or discuss subject Y for fun or entertainment, if it makes your colleagues uncomfortable, it is in the end incompatible with professionalism. This injunction against discomfort of course doesn't prohibit challenging but important conversations, for example about justice or inclusion.

Finally, a practical observation: the stakes are high, and you can easily get yourself fired. When you inch toward your own line, you might already be across someone else's, and regardless of whether your behavior meets a legal definition of harassment, a pattern of discomfiting others won't endear you to your employer. Why risk it?

Alcohol with Colleagues

Just about every fire-able misbehavior I've seen has happened under the influence of alcohol. Drinking with colleagues is, it must be admitted, incredibly fun—you share stress together, and sharing the relief of that stress with alcohol is a universal pleasure (and has been more or less everywhere, more or less forever, as far as I know). When your colleagues are drinking and you aren't, the FOMO can be a bitter pill. I've nevertheless concluded that it's not worth the risk of damage to reputation or even career-ending misbehavior. Just three of the many risks are

1. Making an unwanted sexual advance to a colleague

2. Saying something politically incorrect that offends someone

3. Just getting embarrassingly sloppy, for example, throwing up

I've seen all three more than once; I've seen, for example, one colleague drunkenly call another "darling" repeatedly at the office and burst into tears when asked to stop. If you avoid drinking with colleagues, you can be sure that whatever your other failings, you won't do that. If you absolutely must drink with coworkers or at the office, then for goodness' sake just have one.

Communication

A Holistic Look at Engineering Communication

This chapter takes a high-level look at effective engineering communication, aiming to frame later chapters on email, meetings, and presentations.

I'm nothing special as a coder; I work hard and carefully, but I'm slower than the norm and probably not more detail-oriented. Still, I've been welcomed and rewarded more than I deserve on the many teams I've worked on, and I believe it's because I work unusually hard at communication. Even simple projects demand constant communication, but we're terrible at it as an industry, prone to excessive focus on the details, omitting context, and, above all, poor listening. I think that mismatch leaves us starved for clarity, which is an opportunity—in an industry of poor communicators, you can make a peculiar superpower of understanding exactly what people mean and capturing exactly what matters in response.

D. Heller, *Building a Career in Software*, https://doi.org/10.1007/978-1-4842-6147-7_11

Receiving

We forget the obvious: our main goal in listening and reading email is to understand exactly what someone means and why they mean it. This is both a social exercise, an attempt to model the mind of our colleague, and an attention exercise, an attempt to control our desire to talk or daydream and focus on another person. Like coding or writing, some are blessed with a greater gift than others, but it can be cultivated, too; I'll recommend a few techniques in a moment. If we don't succeed in understanding what a collaborator is saying and why they're saying it, it's obvious that we may miss important input to real-world decisions—but it's also worth noting that any effort to persuade or inform them is harder or impossible. Without first understanding our colleagues, we're apt to tell them things they already know or don't care about, to fail to address their concerns, or to fail to persuade them in the terms that matter to them; in short, any goal we have for transmitting information is far harder.

We also have a major secondary goal in listening: building relationships with our colleagues and allowing them the satisfaction of being understood. That might sound new-agey, but people love feeling heard and hate feeling misunderstood (or worse, ignored), and you can make a friend or ally just by showing you respect a colleague enough to listen carefully.

Here are a few suggestions:

- **Summarize**: The most powerful technique for crystallizing our own understanding is summarizing what someone else has said in a single sentence. This serves two purposes: it forces you to distill your own understanding, and it gives you a chance to validate externally. If you get it right, the other party will confirm (and feel affirmed and grateful)—if you're wrong, you find out fast, get a correction, and still show that you're doing your best. A good summary might start with an explicit acknowledgment that you're trying to confirm you've understood someone:

  Just to make sure I've understood: I think you're saying that we shouldn't tackle feature B until we finish feature A, because we can build B more easily on top of A.

- **Shut up**: Try to let people finish in meetings; when reading, read the whole darn email. This is hard, and we all fail from time to time (especially me), but we should get off the ground, dust ourselves off, and try to shut up again. First and foremost, it gives us a chance to hear and learn, but it is also signals respect and humility to our colleagues.

- **Follow-up 1:1**: Asking follow-up questions is constructive and respectful, but distracting others in a meeting or by email often isn't. I liberally follow-up 1:1 in person, chat, or email when I need clarification.

- **Do your homework**: Understanding our colleagues demands extensive context, both general (your domain and its technologies) and specific (your company's systems). You signal respect and improve your comprehension when you research a domain before engaging with a colleague, particularly before asking for help.

- **Ask a thoughtful follow-up question**: For the most part, this is confined to clarifying things you don't understand. In a 1:1 setting, it can be a good opportunity to connect as a fellow human being—showing a genuine human interest in another person is the easiest way to do that. For example, "How do you feel about that?"

Transmitting

Whether in person, on chat, or over email, the central concerns of conveying your ideas are, in approximately priority order

- **Relevance**: Talking about things people care about and minimizing things they don't

- **Context**: Making sure your audience has sufficient background to understand you

- **Clarity**: Capturing the exact idea you see in your mind's eye

- **Efficiency**: Making effective, that is, minimal, use of your audience's time and attention

- **Sensitivity**: Considering your audience's emotional response to what you're going to say, sometimes known as not making people feel bad unless you need to

These concerns exist in perpetual conflict—context can require verbosity, and sensitivity can conflict with the goal of maximal clarity (sometimes you need to add a spoonful of sugar). Combining them is an art refined only be years of practice, and I won't try to offer a general-purpose algorithm here. However, I will give you some questions to ask yourself that can help you stay on course; I ask myself these questions about every nontrivial email I write or presentation I give (really).

Relevance

- Does this person care about what I'm talking about? A product manager likely doesn't care about technical details (but engineers insist on telling them); a project manager is likely most concerned about schedule and staffing implications; a software engineer likely wants to know about your API.

- What does this person need to get done?

- What information from me helps them get it done?

- How does my work help or hurt their goals?

- Am I talking about what *I* care about or what *they* care about (it should probably be the latter!).

- Am I telling my audience something they already know?

Context

- Do my colleagues know the terms I'm using?

- Do they understand the technology well enough to follow my argument?

- Do they know the goals and responsibilities of the key people involved in this issue?

Clarity

- Is my sentence structure simple?

- Am I using appropriately simple language for this audience? Professors may need different language than interns.

- Can my audience hear me? Am I speaking clearly, loudly, and reasonably slowly?

Efficiency

- Could I say less?

- Might they already understand part of this explanation?

- Could I link to some an explanation instead of describing this here?

Sensitivity

- What could my audience be stressed/worried about? How can I reassure them?

- Am I saying anything that might accidentally insult someone else's technology?

- Is anyone involved personally invested in a specific outcome in a way that might make them more or less receptive to what I'm saying?

Asking yourself these questions can help you stay on the right track, but there's also powerful real-time feedback available: your audience's reaction. I've watched countless engineers blunder on when their audience has already signaled that they're bored or bewildered, and while reading your audience isn't always easy, you should be trying. For example:

- What do their questions imply about their understanding of what I'm saying?

- What emotions do I see on their face? Are they confused? Frustrated? Do they have something to say?

- Does their response suggest a fundamental misunderstanding that I can correct or an area where we have a very different model of the world?

- Do they seem impatient with my exposition? Could it be that they understand things better than I thought, or care about something different than I expected?

- Should I change directions or skip part of what I'm planning to say?

Choosing a Medium

When you reach out to a colleague in today's workplace, you can choose between instant messages (a.k.a. "chat"), SMS, email, phone, and videoconference, as well as dropping by in person[1] or scheduling a meeting. Each channel has its own practical trade-offs and subtle social implications; this section will help you choose between them and will offer a few key tips for each. One option, email, is so important that I'll discuss it in its own chapter (Chapter 13). I consider three qualities when deciding how to reach out:

---

[1] *I'm writing this during COVID-19 lockdown, so no one is doing any dropping-by in person whatsoever, but we're all hopeful for the future.*

Sync/async: Synchronous channels, such as in-person questions, interrupt your colleagues, costing them productivity; asynchronous channels, such as email, let them respond at their leisure, making you wait but minimizing disruption. You should respect your colleagues' concentration by going async when you can afford to; excessive interruptions cost social capital (see Chapter 7). However, you may have to choose a more synchronous medium if your subject is urgent or if you need to iterate together, which is too slow otherwise.

Bandwidth: A tiny question can be squeezed into the meager bandwidth of an instant message, while a very complex question demands the richer structure of an email or speed of human voice. An overly complex question in a low-bandwidth channel will frustrate other engineers.

Formality: This quality is a slippery matter of local convention, but important. The more onerous your request, and the greater your colleague's seniority relative to you, the more formal should be your channel (and language). Generally, email > chat > drive-by question.

Let's zoom in on our options.

Email

Fully asynchronous; high bandwidth; formality varies.

Email is the most important medium for office communication, so much so that I have dedicated Chapter 13 to the subject. Email is asynchronous, minimizing disruption to your audience. It's quite compatible with formality, which makes it appropriate for questions to senior colleagues, though that may be overkill for casual discussions with peers. It's by far the easiest way to reach a large audience. Its greatest weakness is lack of interactivity; it tends to be a quite poor way to iterate on complex issues or resolve controversy compared to in-person discussion.

Chat/Instant Messaging

Semi-synchronous; low bandwidth; informal.

Chat is a fast, loose, casual game and a critical part of engineering collaboration. It's great for communication that's informal (low-stakes issues, people you know well), interactive (more back and forth), and semi-synchronous (I need information soon but not immediately), but its low bandwidth makes it a poor choice for capturing real complexity. If you need to carefully marshal a lot of information, email is your friend; if you need to go back and forth at length, you want to use your voice.

The principles for effective chat are similar to those of effective email—favor brevity, arm your audience with context, and reply as quickly as you can. I'll offer three chat-specific tips:

- Many engineers become enraged when someone sends them an opening chat ("hi pete!" or "hi" or "do you have a second") and don't send their actual question at the same time. This doesn't bother me personally one bit, and I don't consider the pet peeve well-founded, but you should stay on the safe side and avoid this pattern by sending your question along with your greeting.

- Decent punctuation is advised; capitalization is not required and may come off a touch stuffy. Emojis are encouraged. I don't know why those are the conventions, and they may change anytime.

- Chat is a poor choice for recording a decision, because decisions should be permanently recorded, easy to search, and subjectively more formal. Don't leave a controversial decision recorded in chat only; use email.

Drive-By Questions (Going to Someone's Desk)

Fully synchronous; high bandwidth; informal.

Walking over to someone's desk interrupts their flow completely; it shouldn't be done lightly. However, when you're stuck and want to work through something tricky with a colleague, it's the way to go. I strongly advise you to always ping by chat first; that way you at least show that you respect your colleague's right to concentration.

- Do you have a moment to chat about how to add an endpoint to the Inventory service? I can also schedule us some time later in the week if that's better.

- Sure, I have time now, what's up?

- OK if I come by your desk?

- Come on over!

Once you're standing over your colleague, you should be looking for the first sensible opportunity to let them get back to work! The engineer who comes by your desk and won't quit talking is a cliché to avoid.

Scheduled Meetings

Asynchronous; high bandwidth; formality varies.

Scheduled meetings are asynchronous (i.e., less disruptive than a drive-by question) and appropriate for complex subjects; they are, however, very costly and should be reserved for cases that really require that level of bandwidth. See Chapter 5 for a discussion of effective meetings.

SMS

Synchronous; low bandwidth; informal.

In my experience, SMS is only used for time-sensitive communication, for example, about paperwork on a deadline, when chat has already failed for some reason. It's great for those cases but too disruptive for nonurgent messages and not synchronous enough for something like an outage, which can tolerate no waiting.

Synchronous Phone Calls

Completely synchronous; high bandwidth; informal.

Similar to SMS, I mostly see synchronous phone calls (i.e., not planned meetings) used for extremely urgent issues, like ongoing outages.

Technical Writing

If there's one skill that will get you moving in software, it's coding. If there are two, the second is architecture, but if there are three, the third is certainly technical writing. We write every single day—emails to our managers, instant messages to ask questions of busy people, manuals for customers, comments in our codebases, design documents, etc., etc., etc., and my personal experience has been that crisp writing can save enormous confusion and make your ideas far more persuasive. It also has a less obvious benefit—good writing is unreasonably impressive to most engineers and managers and can build your reputation.

We'll start with eight foundational principles common to all technical writing before elaborating on good document structure and the process of editing.

- **Be concise**: Anything that doesn't clarify obfuscates. Holding precision constant, take out absolutely everything that doesn't improve the reader's understanding. Can you remove a word? Can you remove a paragraph?

- **Emphasize conclusions**: Readers usually care most about high-level conclusions; make those crystal clear, and don't drown the reader in details. Lead with a tl;dr!

D. Heller, *Building a Career in Software*, https://doi.org/10.1007/978-1-4842-6147-7_12

- **Put yourself in your readers' place**: Ask yourself what matters to them, what they know, and whether they will understand what you've written.

- **Guide readers with clear structure**: Clear structure helps readers follow your writing. It's often best to start with an introduction/summary, follow with clearly titled sections addressing specific areas, and close with a conclusion. Use bulleted lists liberally.

- **Use simple language**: The simplest language that will convey your meaning is usually the best choice for readability. Any terminology that is not highly likely to be known to the reader should be replaced or defined; is the reader going to understand the technical term you're about to use?

- **Provide ample context**: When you introduce an idea or piece information, the reader should already have the context they need to reason about it, and you should explain its relevance immediately; otherwise, it will confuse them.

- **Lead with your most important points**: Writing, from sentences to paragraphs to whole books, is usually clearest when it leads with its most important points.

- **Edit for precision**: Precision may be the highest virtue in technical communication; reread your writing and ask, does it say *exactly* what I mean?

For engineers, the two most common problems are failing to provide enough context (assuming the reader knows everything you know) and giving too much detail (forgetting that the reader doesn't care about everything you do), so if you do your very best to resist those temptations, you're off to a good start.

A Note About Structure

With every word we pile on a busy, stressed-out reader, we chip away at their finite attention and sense of direction; they will abandon ship unless we get our point across early and constantly refresh their interest and energy. Our structural tools to do that are

- A razor-sharp introduction that summarizes everything else. Our introduction makes sure that our readers want to read everything that follows and understand its purpose; it should ensure that if readers give up early, they'll still walk away with the most important points.

- Sections delineated by headers or paragraph breaks.

- Section ordering that sorts first for comprehensibility—necessary context first—and then by importance—most important points in early, before the reader gives up.

Our introduction is our most important section. It catches the reader's attention and creates momentum; it should give them something to remember if they quit before the end, which many people will.

Each clearly marked section after should be a landmark that reminds the reader where they are in the universe; you'll find my best efforts at following this principle throughout this book, including in this chapter!

When you're finally done writing all your sections, you're not done—you're ready to edit.

Editing

Editing is a painful process, a fine art, and the subject of many books better than this one. Its concept is simple: reread your work, find things to improve, and fix them. We can edit at both the micro level—improving each sentence one by one—and at the macro level—improving overall organization and content.

The microscale improvements are easier, so I suggest you start there and use that process to discover bigger problems. This process is a while loop: we start at the top of our document, read every sentence, improve each one, and repeat until we simply cannot improve any more.

For each sentence, you can apply all eight principles from earlier. If nothing else, you can ask

1. Can I take out words?

2. Can I write a simpler sentence?

3. Is there enough context?

```
while text.couldBeBetter():
    for sentence in text:
        sentence.removeWords()
        sentence.simplify()

        if sentence.missingContext():
            text.goBackAndAddContext()
```

Remove Words

This is the simplest, easiest, and by far the most effective editing technique of which I know; we go back through our text and reread every single sentence we've written, identify all the words we've added that aren't strictly necessary, and take them out (or, in some cases, simplify). Here's an example.

This is the simplest, ~~easiest,~~[1] and ~~by far the~~[2] most effective editing technique ~~of which~~[3] I know; we ~~go back through our text and~~[4] reread every ~~single~~[5] sentence ~~we've written,~~[6] identify ~~all the words we've added that aren't strictly necessary~~[7] **unnecessary words**, and ~~take out (or, in some cases, simplify)~~[8] **remove** them.

This is the most effective editing technique I know; we reread every sentence, identify unnecessary words, and remove them.

---

1. **"Easiest"**: "Simple" gets the idea across on its own, people will figure out that it's easy.

2. **"Most effective"**: Is plenty strong, "by far" is gratuitous.

3. **"Of which"**: Adds no information.

4. **"Reread"**: Already implies going back through the text.

5. **"Every single"**: This phrase is stronger than "every," but we don't seem to need to be strong here.

6. **"We've written"**: We already know that we wrote the text.

7. **"All the words we've added that aren't strictly necessary"**: We can be more direct and briefer at the same time with "unnecessary words."

8. **"... take out (or, in some cases, simplify)"**: We pay a small amount of information, but we buy back quite a lot of words.

We've reduced our word count from 52 to 21, saving our readers' precious time and energy for more valuable purposes, like reasoning about our ideas. This technique is both easy and effective—the return on investment is extremely high, so make it your #1 editing technique. I wouldn't send any written communication out the door without a word removal pass.

Simplify Sentences

There are plenty of widely quoted grammar rules out there, and many of them turn out to be nonsense.[1] I'll offer only one opinion: when in doubt, write short sentences where one subject does one action on one thing, in that order.

> *<Subject> <Action> <Object>. <Subject> <Action> <Object>.*
>
> *The infrastructure team is migrating the data to the cloud. This migration blocks big schema changes. They expect to finish by the end of the week, and we can launch this feature at that time.*

We're simple, maybe to a fault, but you know what I'm talking about; the last sentence is actually two such sentences stitched together with an "and" but preserves the Subject-Action-Object structure and is still simple to read. Compare with the following mush:

> *We can launch this feature after the infrastructure team finishes the migration of the database to the cloud, which blocks big schema changes but should be finished by the end of the week.*

Get the Context Right

Managing context is more slippery than our previous two methods. Removing words and simplifying sentence structure can be done one sentence at a time, almost one word at a time, a kind of peephole optimizer. Tuning context demands that we model our own minds and our readers', understanding the knowledge and assumptions hidden under our writing and sensing when our readers won't share them. We can ask:

- Does the reader know everything they need to know to understand what I've said?

- Will the reader believe me, or do I need to justify myself?

- Am I explaining something the reader already understands?

For financial transaction data, we will need greater consistency than OurDistributedDataStore guarantees. Therefore, those records will be stored in OurReplicatedACIDDatabase, which should offer sufficient throughput for this workload. Our application will be written in Java, which supports Object Oriented Programming; inheritance will allow good code reuse.

---

[1] If you need a hand down off your high passive voice horse, or help accepting that split infinitives are no problem at all, I recommend Steven Pinker's *The Sense of Style*.

The consistency and performance of distributed databases are notoriously subtle; almost any audience will need some clarification. Even if the reader knows exactly how OurDistributedDataStore works, they probably don't know exactly what guarantees the financial transaction data needs; we should tell them. As for OurReplicatedACIDDatabase, the reader probably understands that it's super-consistent, but will they trust that the throughput is high enough without any evidence? Finally, we have an error in the opposite direction—our audience is programmers, and telling them how Java OOP works is condescending (that's a real example that I saw happen last week!).

For financial transaction data, we will need greater consistency than OurDistributedDataStore guarantees; account balances for each user must be stored in separate rows, and transfers between them must be atomic. OurDistributedDataStore can only guarantee consistency for transactions on a single row. Therefore, those records will be stored in OurReplicatedACIDDatabase. While it does not offer the same throughput, we have load tested it up to 15,000 transactions per second, 10x the maximum projected QPS in 1 region.

Even careful writers will sometimes explain too much or not enough; when you're deep in a subject, it's hard to tell the difference. Once you've edited your little heart out, you can stop modeling other people's minds and ask a real live colleague for feedback.

Spelling, Grammar, Capitalization, and Punctuation

I've known many effective and admired engineers and managers who write with poor spelling, grammar, and punctuation; it isn't any kind of deal-breaker. Still, I advise you to get things right if you can; not just because I'm old-fashioned but because I think errors are just a little bit distracting and their absence makes a more professional impression.

Spelling is easy in this day and age—trust your spellchecker and double-check meanings in a dictionary if you're not 100% sure of a word. Pay attention when your Word processor shows you red.

Punctuation and capitalization aren't too bad either—start sentences with capitals, end them with periods, and you're doing pretty well. Commas, colons, and semicolons are error-prone little tricksters, but Google Docs can often flag a mistake.

Grammar overall, though, is a messy business, without an accessible reference or trustworthy technology that I know of (though you can Google for every answer under the sun if you can come up with the right question). Therefore, your best friend is reading out loud to see if a sentence sounds natural; your second-best friend is a trustworthy editor who can take a look for you.

Redis is quite efficient for small payload sizes, but it can degrade significantly for larger objects	We need a comma because both halves have a subject ("Redis", "it") and a verb ("is", "can")
Cassandra is optimized for high write volume but can struggle with heavy read traffic	We don't need a comma, because the second half ("can struggle with heavy read traffic") doesn't have a subject

Effective Email

This chapter is a comprehensive guide to professional engineering email. We'll cover organizing information, but we'll also discuss subjects like selecting an audience, tuning your level of formality, formatting, how to show respect, and small-but-nonobvious details like addressing and signing. First: motivation.

You're going to write a lot of email as a software engineer, and if you're lucky, you'll read only ten times as much; if you're really lucky, some of it won't be terrible. You'll read every variety of bad email: emails that are way too long, emails packed with useless detail, confusing emails without enough context, off-topic replies, and emails that make enemies for no good reason. Above all, you'll read irrelevant emails that should never have been sent.

I'm a slow emailer, endlessly revising and agonizing over every word, preoccupied with all the above traps; I've often spent a whole morning on a single delicate message. Still, I've found that investing in effective email pays for itself many times over in project results and reputation—results because projects go better when your collaborators know what's going on and what you need from them, and reputation because engineers, focused on code rather than humans, find good email a mystical skill.

The Art of Sending and Not Sending Email

Email is still technical writing (Chapter 12), and my best advice is therefore to write briefly and clearly. If all you do is follow the advice of that chapter, you'll be above average: emphasize your conclusions, edit for brevity and precision, focus on what your readers care about, and remember what they know and don't. That said, email demands many small decisions irrelevant to a stand-alone technical document.

© Daniel Heller 2020
D. Heller, *Building a Career in Software*, https://doi.org/10.1007/978-1-4842-6147-7_13

Structure

Emails have simple structure; you'll probably have it down after reading your first few hundred work emails. We have a salutation (or opening), an optional tl;dr, a series of body sections, some kind of closing, and a signature. The overriding concerns are brevity and clarity, so I encourage you to make paragraph/section breaks and bulleted lists liberally (to a point—bullets can become hard to parse if they break apart material that naturally goes together).

Hi SRE Team (cc Dhivya, Jeff from Storage),

tl;dr Centralized DB tracing rolls out tomorrow; view your instance's logs at dbtracing.ourcompany.com. In an emergency, disable tracing in the config flag system at config.ourcompany.com/tracingprop.

Starting tomorrow, we'll be rolling out centralized tracing for our MySQL instances. Logs are aggregated in Elasticsearch and can be viewed per-instance on dbtracing.ourcompany.com.

The log extraction is based on Filebeat and is expected to be minimally invasive, but in an emergency, it can be disabled per-instance by setting enabled to "false" at config.ourcompany.com/tracingprop. If you have an urgent need to increase verbosity, you can update the log level there as well.

We'll send an update when this rollout is complete. Feedback and questions are welcome and appreciated. Thanks to Dhivya and Jeff for their hard work to make this possible!

Cheers,

DH

Salutation: whom you're writing, possibly calling out the people you're directly addressing and those you're merely keeping in the loop separately. Followed by a comma

Optional tl;dr:

Body Section 1 of N: most important points if possible, should frame everything else

Body section 2 of N: more detail; striving to cover only one subject per section, in this case operational concerns

Optional closing: an opportunity to prepare for future communication, reiterate important points, show respect, and give credit

Signature: purely a formality in the email age but obligatory to avoid undue informality

---

Salutations

Most business emails today begin with

Hi <person or group>,

That is, "Hi," some identifier for the addressee, and a comma. Historically, we often used colons to terminate salutations in business emails, but this is fading—use commas. The first character is always capitalized, and names are always capitalized; groups may or may not be.

Hi Apoorva,

Hi Amaliya and Jeremy,

Hi migration team, // Looks a bit informal, but can be acceptable

Hi folks,

When addressing a small- to medium-sized group, the preferred form is "Hi folks."[1] "Guys," previously used in the gender-neutral plural, is now widely considered as sexist and should be avoided entirely in business contexts. For larger groups, you can use "Hi everyone" or "Hi all." The most complex form you'll need to use on a regular basis is when addressing one group but CCing another—for example, if you mail the web team but want to inform the back-end team. In that case, you should make it clear whom you're CCing in parenthesis; this lets others replying adjust their replies for the audience.

Hi web folks (cc Chen and Mike),

For very short emails to close collaborators, you may omit the salutation, but I almost always include it to avoid sounding curt.

Finally, when in doubt, mirror what's already been used on a thread!

Signatures

You have four options for signing an email:

Just your name: This is fairly informal, appropriate for fast, efficient conversations between peers. I wouldn't address a superior this way, and I find it a bit short for strangers. This might be the right closing for an email that also doesn't need a salutation.

Sounds great to me!

DH

---

[1] "Folks" is not a proper noun, so it should not be capitalized. However, people do often capitalize it, and I've never seen anyone object.

Cheers: This is a friendly, cheerful signature appropriate to an email between peers who might not be on such familiar terms that you want to end without a signature at all. It's also appropriate to large lists with a variety of people on them.

Hi everyone,

This plan sounds good to me! Let's run with it.

Cheers,

DH

Thanks: This is just slightly more formal than "cheers" but can be used in more or less the same circumstances (especially when you're thanking people!). It's an appropriate signature for large lists within your company, superiors, senior colleagues, and colleagues within your company you don't know well.

Regards or best: These are the most formal, appropriate to business interactions between people from different companies, especially if you haven't worked together extensively. We generally use the most formality when going outside of our own company or across major branches of a company; they'll sound stilted in normal internal mail but are more or less the only option for initial interactions across firms.

Hi Maria,

Sounds good to me! I'll meet you and your team in our lobby on Tuesday at 11AM.

Best,

Dan // Note use of my n*ame, rather than my initials/nickname*

The Importance of TL;DR

tl;dr Many readers don't have time to read every word of your email, especially executives. Start your emails with an ultra-brief summary in boldface.

tl;dr means "Too Long, Didn't Read"—a snarky response to a long Internet post. In a professional context, it refers to an ultra-brief summary of an email or document, placed upfront for people who want to know what's up but don't have the time or appetite for every word. Some emails are only two sentences or go to a single recipient who does care about every word. In that case, skip a tl;dr. Most emails, though, go to larger audiences, and lots of those readers are going to be short on time—most importantly, that includes executives, whose calendars are horror movies and who almost never need to know the details. Almost any email with complex content and a large audience, especially technical announcements, should offer those readers an ultra-condensed summary, set in bold and explicitly labeled tl;dr.

Replying On Topic

Every week I see engineers and managers reply embarrassingly off-topic to clear questions. This may sound obvious, but irrelevant responses come off poorly and, more importantly, are frustrating to question askers ("now I need to reply to that whole thread and ask the same question again!"). Read, read, and read again, model the mind of your correspondent, ask yourself what exactly is this person asking, ask for clarification 1:1 if you need it, and then, finally, reply magnificently on topic.

Large Mailing Lists

Large mailing lists are high-risk, low-reward. It's easy to embarrass yourself with a stupid question (yes, they exist) or the wrong tone but rare to impress or sway people enough to justify that risk; therefore, I almost never send a message to a large list, and I advise you to do the same. You can usually get the same rewards at a fraction of the risk by talking to someone 1:1 or tracking down a smaller mailing list.

That said, there are (rare) times to hit reply-all to a few hundred people—say, someone asks for help with a problem that many people have, and you're (for some reason) the only one who knows the answer. When you do reply-all, it should be with super-premium content, material of great technical interest and utility to the audience, presented with a positive attitude and respect, polished to a mirror shine of good spelling, structure, and grammar—we put only our best foot forward.

Once in a great, great while—once in five years or even less often—tremendous conviction may shove you into making a controversial point (also with a positive attitude, respect, and humility). I have literally never felt the need, and if you do, you're probably wrong. Walk away and think about it.

Whatever the complexities of that decision, let me offer one iron rule—never, ever, ever reply to a large list in anger or with disrespect; you're hurting your own reputation and dignity far more than you're helping your cause or gratifying yourself, and you just might find a way to get yourself fired (I've seen it happen). There are no exceptions.

Etiquette, Formality, and Polish

Every word of your emails lives forever, striped to a thousand GMail servers; they're ready to be reread with growing anger, forwarded to managers, quoted to HR, and discovered in lawsuits. In short—behave yourself over email. All of Chapter 6's lessons about manners apply doubly to email. Here are three tips to remember:

1. Never, ever show anger or disparage another person over email, even 1:1 to someone you trust; emails have a way of getting forwarded. You're going to have moments when you write angry emails; save the draft, walk away, and come back when you're ready to delete it.

2. Scale your formality with your audience, erring toward more when in doubt—emails to your best friend at the office can be unsigned one-liners, but emails to your VP should be pristine. Overdoing it can be stiff, drastically overdoing it can be tone-deaf, but usually erring toward more formality shows that you take your audience seriously.

3. Looping in stakeholders shows respect; try to include people who have a reason to care about your subject so they don't feel that business takes place behind their back.

The Importance of Links

Technical emails inevitably reference data and require heaps of context. Visionaries have blessed us with the perfect tool to assist our readers: the hyperlink. The more your readers have to strain to find the context to understand your email, the less they'll understand it and the more annoying they'll find it and you—but an in-line link for every mystery can keep you in their good graces. Reference an endpoint's success rate? Link directly to the dashboard. Reference a system that not everyone may know? Link to its wiki page. Reference a feature of a database or language? Link to its documentation. All of the above can save your readers time, energy, and cognitive load. It's doubly important for assertions that may be controversial; resolve your readers' doubt as quickly as possible.

"Remove Me From This List"

Maybe this section can save you some embarrassment and fight an epidemic ravaging America's companies—the "please remove me from this list" reply. Around once a month, you're going to see an accidental email to a huge mailing list that you didn't know you were on. You're also going to see 15 people—literally 15—reply to the entire company saying, "I don't work on this, please remove me from this list." This is a mystery to me and others, because I've never once seen an email list you could unsubscribe from by replying to the entire list. Maybe you can unsubscribe manually in a Google Groups page, maybe you can email the list administrator, whatever—all I know is that replying to 10,000 employees won't get you there.

Email Archetypes

This section will present templates for a few common emails you may find yourself sending. These aren't the only options in these contexts, but if you follow these formats, at least in 2020, no one will look at you askance.

The Technical Announcement

Technical announcements start with a tl;dr, follow-up with more detailed explanations of their backstories, embed many links for context, and usually invite feedback and offer help.

Hi <group>,

tl;dr <thing is happening>. <people will experience some impact>

<background and motivation>

<thing is happening>

<summary implications for readers; what they really need to do; links to more detail>

<invite feedback and offer help>

For example:

Hi all,

tl;dr SingleDB is deprecated for analytics; all analytics will be ingested to Snowflake by way of Kafka (using the AnalyticsClient). We have <u>documentation</u> for creating tables, emitting metrics, and backfilling data. The deadline to migrate is the end of Q2.

SingleDB has been our storage system for all data, including analytics, since the company's inception. As we've started to produce a greater variety and volume of analytics, we want to move those data off of our production database to reduce interference with customer traffic, improve cost efficiency, and enable integrations with various warehousing tools.

Therefore, we are moving to storing analytics in Snowflake. Data will be logged to Kafka using our internal AnalyticsClient, then ingested to Snowflake from there. The steps for migrating data are:

Configure tables and ingestion in the warehouse as discussed <u>here</u>.

Adopt the AnalyticsClient to dual-write data. The client is already available in the monorepo. An example usage can be found <u>here</u>.

Backfill data as discussed <u>here</u>.

Remove existing writes to SingleDB.

This process is documented overall <u>here</u>. Our org-wide target to complete this migration is the end of Q2, and we intend migrations for feature teams to be quite easy. If you need help with this migration or have any concerns, please don't hesitate to reach out to data-team@ourcompany.com. Thanks in advance for your help completing this migration!

Thanks,

DH on behalf of the Data Team

The Technical Question

You can use the principles from Chapter 14 to craft technical questions.

The Operational Risk

As discussed in "Bus Factor > 1" (Chapter 20), when we discover information of operational significance, we email it to our team. Here's the template for doing so:

Hi folks,

tl;dr <tl;dr>

We've just become aware that <technical issue>. This implies that <operational risk>. <operator guidance>. We are working on a fix and will keep this list updated. Please reach out with any questions.

<signature>

For example:

Hi folks,

tl;dr App restarts are causing errors; please only restart if absolutely necessary.

We've just become aware that an issue in our load balancing configuration is causing user-visible errors when recommendation service instances are restarted. Zi and I are actively investigating, but in the short term, please do not deploy or restart unless absolutely necessary. Please reach out with any questions.

Thanks,

DH

The Project Status Update

People who care about projects usually care about two things: schedule (when things will be done) and downstream implications (how they can or must use them). That's true for almost everyone you'll need to update, from close technical collaborators to managers to VPs.

However, they'll care about different levels of abstraction: leaders and distant stakeholders (say, the whole company) will care about the project level, that is, how the whole thing is going and the impact on stakeholders. Close collaborators like your project teammates will care about the details, the exact functionality you've built, and what they can do with it.

You can either pick one level of abstraction (say, if you're only emailing your closest collaborators) or combine both—starting with the high level but including more detail below. In both cases, you'll break down your update by subprojects, covering

1.   Project background

2.   Progress

3.   Impact on stakeholders

4.   Schedule

5.   Plans

6.   Issues

The template:

Hi <audience>,

<project summary or background link> <key changes>. <overall status/schedule>. <any important announcements>.

Area 1: progress, impact, schedule, plans, problems

...

Area N: progress, impact, schedule, plans, problems

Thanks!

<you>

For example, an update to a large engineering list:

Hi folks,

The Snowflake migration (proposal) is estimated to be on track for completion by the end of next month. This month, we released the EventCompare tool that can compare events in the legacy system to tables in the warehouse; please use this tool to verify your migrations.

Event migrations: 16 of our 25 event types have been fully migrated, including deleting legacy event logging code. Follow our progress in this tracker.

Query migrations: all analytics UIs have been updated to support reading from either legacy tables or the new warehouse. See this doc for configuration.

Tooling: EventCompare was released to enable verification of new warehouse tables against legacy data. This tool has been used by four teams to verify updates.

As always, questions and feedback are welcome at data-team@ourcompany.com.

Cheers,

DH on behalf of the Data team

In contrast, we might update a manager on a small slice of that project with a shorter, less structured email that still describes progress, acknowledges a small issue, describes the remaining work, and estimates the schedule.

Hi Umesh,

Quick update on progress this week. I've merged my PRs to emit history-page analytics to Kafka and do the Snowflake ingestion. EventCompare helped me catch one small bug, but after that fix things are looking pretty good, and the backfill is running now. I want to let this run for another week before deleting the legacy code, but I think we can likely mark this completed early in the week after next (the 22nd or 23rd).

Cheers,

DH

Finally, we might informally update close collaborators who know almost every detail of what we're doing, focusing on fine-grained detail.

Hi Brandon and Jing,

I'm almost ready with the fix for the conflict-handling bug in the backfill tool; I plan to have a PR ready for you to review tomorrow. After that, I'll start on the observability improvements we talked about, which should take the rest of the week, because I realized I'll need to do small refactor first. Brandon, do you think you could take a look at the errors Sarah reported?

Cheers,

DH

Requesting a Meeting

When requesting a meeting from someone whose help we need, our main goals are respect and efficiency—show that you appreciate your help, and, to the extent possible, save them effort and confusion of any kind except showing up to dispense their wisdom.

We start with a concise sentence or two of background explaining who we are and what we're working on; otherwise they'll be confused (and therefore annoyed). We continue with a request for a meeting, explaining what we hope to discuss and accomplish. Finally, we touch on logistics; particularly, if you have the benefit of a shared calendaring system, you offer to take care of scheduling the meeting.

Here's a template for a meeting request to someone you don't know who works at the same company.

Hi <person>:

I'm on <team> and am currently working on <project>. Right now, I'm <working on part of project>, and <some reason to seek out their help came up>. [I realize you may not be the right person for this question; if I'm wrong, sincere apologies! Otherwise...][2] Would you mind if I schedule a brief meeting to <achieve specific goal>? Thanks so much!

Cheers,

<you>

For example:

Hi Simon,

I'm on the platform team and am currently working on our migration from Thrift to gRPC. Right now, the tooling is in a beta state, and we're ready to start onboarding our first services.

We're thinking that the inventory services might be a good place to start, since they're using the newest versions of the RPC framework. Amy said that you have some of the best expertise in those services; would you mind if I schedule a brief meeting to discuss whether this is a good place to start, and if so, pick a first service? Thanks!

---

[2]Include this sentence if and only if you actually have uncertainty about who the right person to talk to is. If you are wrong, it's annoying, and you should make it clear that you don't take that lightly.

Cheers,

DH

The Intro Email

When introducing two people so they can collaborate in some way, we address them both in turn, providing context on the other party, then finish with a standard note about BCCing yourself (so they can continue the conversation privately).

Hi <A> and <B>,

<A>: <B> is <B's relationship to you>, <background>, <optional quip>. <Reason for connecting you>

<B>: <A> is <A's relationship to you>, <background>, <optional quip>. <Reason for connecting you>

I'll leave you two to connect and move me to BCC. Hope you can catch up soon!

<signature>

For example:

Hi Ramesh and Wei,

Ramesh: Wei is a long-time colleague of mine on the Infrastructure team, an experienced network engineer, and all around hacker. She's considering making a move to the StartupWithinAStartup team (that's still not public knowledge) and wants to learn more about the team.

Wei: Ramesh and I worked together at FooCorp and then on the Security team right after I joined. He's worked on the StartupWithinAStartup team for the last two years and has good insight into how the team operates.

I'll leave you two to connect and move me to BCC. Hope you can catch up soon!

Cheers,

DH

Email Strategy

In most software jobs, you'll receive a crushing volume of email—status updates, overly polished newsletters, 50 kinds of auto-generated reports and notifications, threads on large mailing lists, and, of course, the occasional request that really requires a response.

You'll need a strategy for managing this deluge—for efficiently acquiring the information you need, discarding what you don't, losslessly responding to what needs responding, and protecting enough time and focus to produce technology.

Keep Your Inbox Empty

Many engineers practice Inbox Zero, a strategy for managing the flood by keeping one's inbox nearly empty. The strategy calls for acting on every email in one way or another in processing sessions, aiming to conclusively resolve most either by replying, archiving, or forwarding, and removing others from sight in a special folder for deferred processing if needed.

I don't follow this method in all its details, but it's well worth researching and considering. I did adopt what I personally consider its most important principle—I regularly drain my inbox all the way to zero, and I strongly advise you to do the same. This practice has two important benefits: first, you will never permanently miss an email because it is buried under a lot of junk you don't care about, and second, it will give you a subjective sense of triumph over your email, flushing away the feeling that you have an ungovernable haystack to sort through and countless important emails you're missing. I consider this more or less a special case of getting things done—fighting cognitive load and stress by ensuring that confidence that your system will always surface important action items. When you oblige yourself to act on every single email, you avoid the stress of whether you missed something.

Reduce Your Inbound

If you don't need to read it, you should never see it. Companies are constantly creating mailing lists for every manner of automatic notifications, and most of them can be safely ignored. I find that it's quite easy to spam-creep your way into spending your whole day archiving junk. The moment you recognize that a list isn't necessary, you should send it directly to your archive or trash can.

Folders (Mostly) Don't Help

When I first started getting a lot of email, my strategy was to route it into many topic-based folders and review those folders one by one. This made my problems much worse. Consuming all my mail required countless individual steps, I missed important mail as a result, and I felt a vague sense that I was constantly in the wrong folder, reading the wrong thing, and about to be scolded. This may be a good strategy for strictly optional mail—your newsletters and your semi-relevant updates, which you can easily miss—but you should not employ it for anything important. Send mail to your inbox and vigorously drain the queue—it's the only way to be absolutely sure you haven't missed something important.

I'll note just one important exception: if your company's email system doesn't have powerful search functionality, you may have to do your own organizing after reading to support revisiting important messages.

Emails and To Dos

Email is not the place to keep your to-do list, because you'll have to reexamine long-running to dos again and again and again, wasting your attention and subtly telling yourself again and again that you've failed to do them. As Getting Things Done argues, you should be pulling from the head of your queue with confidence and never frittering away your attention on things you aren't going to do. Track your to dos in a dedicated app.

Email Cadence: The Power and Cost of Fast Replies

When you reply to an email instantly, it's startling and delightful to your correspondent—their normal agonies of impatience evaporate, and you seem a paragon of dedication and energy.

On the other hand, constantly checking your email drags on your energy and focus—I don't think it's possible to write tricky code with constant email breaks.

I'll offer you a few email schedules I've known colleagues to use, then describe my own dubious (but apparently maintainable) pseudo-system.

Some people use radically minimalist systems, like responding to email exactly once a day at the end of the day. I think this is admirable for coding productivity, and maybe it will work for you in your environment. I personally don't think it's acceptable to impose a p50 latency of 12 hours on my colleagues; I check more often.

Some people have disciplined systems for distributing processing throughout the day—for example, processing email at the top of the hour every hour. The argument for this system is that it both caps reply latency and limits interrupts. To me it seems sensible, but I can't manage it—when I'm deep in something, the context switch is too painful.

My experience is that I have two kinds of productive email processing sessions, and I use both during the day:

- The focused session, where I set out to drain the queue completely, send my more complex or tricky messages, and process a cornucopia of inanities.

- The casual glance, where I process at most a couple of emails and see what's doing literally right now (e.g., if someone has hit a serious problem I can help with). I may take the opportunity to try to surprise a colleague with a quick reply or promote the glance to a full session if something urgent and complex comes up.

The focused session demands an expanse of dedicated time, just like complex coding; it's hard to start, hard to resume, and productive. The "glance" can be finely time-sliced, for example, while waiting for a long test suite to run.

My personal system is a focused session in the morning most mornings, then "glances" when I finish something or have a long waiting period in the course of my normal work (I do plenty of three-minute builds). I don't hold myself to a high bar in my "glance" sessions—I try to shoot off a quick reply or two, process and archive what I can, and not get too deep into it. It's a way to decrease latency for critical issues and gift colleagues a few unexpectedly swift replies.

I think doing my focused reading in the evening would actually be better for my productivity, because I do my best work fresh in the morning; when I'm in coding crunch time, I get straight down to it every morning. However, I find evening reading too psychologically difficult to systematize, because when I'm deep into my afternoon coding, it hurts to stop.

Describing Problems and Asking Questions

You will have thousands of occasions in your career to ask technical questions or make other requests of technologists; these are wonderful opportunities to annoy the living daylights out of people you respect or, equally, opportunities to impress. Your principles should be

1. Try a *reasonable amount*[1] to help yourself before you take others' time.

2. Provide ample context, as you would with any other form of technical writing:

---

[1] I haven't yet seen a good general-purpose definition for this reasonable amount; just do your best to consider helping yourself with due consideration of the urgency of your issue.

© Daniel Heller 2020

D. Heller, *Building a Career in Software*, https://doi.org/10.1007/978-1-4842-6147-7_14

- **Your intentions**: What you're trying to do so your colleague knows why you're asking and can decide whether the question is the right one to ask in context.

- **Your observations**: Things that you have seen with your own eyes, as described in *Knowing Our Limits* (Chapter 7). Data that can be used for meaningful inference.

3. Express your question as precisely as you can: you should aim for some sort of actionability, no matter the nature of your question; your collaborator should be able to answer or act on the question as completely as possible based solely on what you've captured.

Here's a bad question that you'll see asked a hundred times:

I saw a problem deploying this service. Do you know what might be wrong?

Here's a much better question:

I've been trying since 1 PM to deploy a logging change to the User Service (commit f752e2ee8) with the Prod Deploy Jenkins job. I see that the job fails, and there's an error message in the Jenkins logs about artifactory not accepting a connection. I think the job is configured correctly—do you know how to check whether artifactory is healthy?

Maybe you're not at all familiar with how to get at the job logs (or some other part of the chain of analysis); you can still ask a more precise and actionable question than "help." Here's another fine question:

I've been trying since 1 PM to deploy a logging change to the User Service with the Prod Deploy Jenkins job. I see in the UI that the job fails, but I've never used Jenkins before, and I'm not sure how to find the logs. Can you walk me through how you'd normally debug an issue like this?

Actually, molding beautifully precise questions is an art that must be mastered over time. Luckily, I think the majority of technical questions can be expressed clearly with one of a few simple "magic templates" that naturally bundle up context in the question.

Magic Template: Asking for Help Debugging

The template:

I'm trying to **<goal>**. I'm doing **<actions>**, but I see **<observations>**. My best theory is **<theory>**, because **<reason>**. Can you **<do something specific>**?

Example:

Hi Shahrooz,

I'm trying to add a new endpoint for kittens to the cat service; the diff is here. I've added the handler to handlers.js and am running the service locally with "make run-local" as per this doc, but when I try to query the new endpoint with curl -v localhost:8888/kittens/tabby, it fails with a 404 and an empty body. I don't see logs from my endpoint in the log browser. I'm wondering whether I missed a step to add the endpoint. Does anything jump out at you that I may have missed? If not, do you mind reviewing the diff with me? I can set us up some time. Thanks!

Cheers,

DH

Let's break it down.

> **<goal>**: Why you're trying to do this thing at all (maybe they know a better approach!).

> **<actions>**: The exact steps that led you to what eventually happened. This lets them construct a mental model of the state of the world at the time of the observation; it also shows that you've really tried to tackle the problem on your own (see *Just Do Something* in Chapter 5).

> **<observation>**: What you saw with your own two eyes. Armed also with the knowledge of what they did to get there, they can now theorize as to why it's happening.

> **<theory> <reason>**: What you've reasoned through so far, which may be important to explain why you've come to this specific person for help. If you don't have

any theories, you can say that. It also shows your helper that you've attempted to reason about the problem on your own.

<do something specific>: You should come with the most actionable request you can, not just explain the situation and stop. That request may be as general as, "can you please look at the logs with me and see if you see anything," but it should be something the other person can act on; you're both giving them the last piece of the context and showing that you're not trying to hand off initiative like a child to a parent ("here I am! Do my work!") but rather have a well-reasoned purpose in taking their time.

You've explained what you want, what you truly know, what you merely suspect, and what exactly you want your colleague to do; you've included links to key background so they could swiftly answer any obvious questions about your story. They're amply armed with context and ready to help, even if that means suggesting an overall new approach to your problem.

Magic Template: Asking For Help with a Production Issue

The template:

We're observing **<observation>** starting at **<time with time zone>**. It is likely causing **<experience>** for **<percentage>** of **<class of users>**. We think **<theory>** and want help **<doinglinvestigating>** **<thing> to mitigate>**.

Example:

We're observing elevated errors on the log-in endpoint starting at 12.30 PM PT. It's likely causing as many as 30% of all customers to fail to log in right now. We've seen log messages about query failures and suspect the database might be struggling. We'd like to ask you to join the video conference and take a look at the DB.

Explanation:

The fundamentals are the same as for any debugging question. However, there are some key additions.

> **\<experience\> \<percentage\> \<class of users\>**: Other systems operators need to understand exactly what the *business impact* of an issue is to reason about risks and benefits of actions, which must include understanding what users are affected and how.

> **\<time with time zone\>**: Understanding impact and correlating events require knowing how long the problem has gone on, and since people may be distributed across time zones, you do well to *always* include them.

Magic Template: Everything Else

You get the idea. Say what you're doing, say what you're seeing, say what you think, and ask for the most specific action you can.

The template:

I'm trying to **\<do a thing\>**. I **\<have done some things I already know some things\>**. To move forward, I want to **\<do or know something else\>**. **\<specific question\>**.

Public Speaking

Public speaking is a regular part of our jobs as technologists, for purposes like training junior colleagues, persuading teams to follow our recommendations, and sharing knowledge with peers. Like writing, public speaking is foreign and alarming to many engineers, which makes it a special opportunity to impress your colleagues and build your reputation; I advise you to seek out as many opportunities to give talks as you can, because practice is the only way to improve (conditional of course on having a subject of interest for your audience).

Below are techniques I use to prepare and deliver my own presentations. You'll find that they overlap with the principles of technical writing and with good reason—your goal is in both cases to engage and entertain your audience, communicate something valuable to them with the greatest possible clarity, and use their time effectively. I encourage you to find more resources on the subject, but I've gotten by fine on the following.

Start with a brief anecdote, humorously delivered if possible: Take your audience's attention right away; it'll be easier to hold than regain. The anecdote should be topical, not just funny—it should explain why you're interested in the subject or why they should be.

Have a clear purpose: You should know what you want your audience to walk away with, and right after your anecdote, you should tell them exactly what that is.

Organize your talk into clear sections: Just as with writing, a clear structure helps your audience contextualize and understand what you're saying at any given moment in your talk. I recommend an agenda slide early.

D. Heller, *Building a Career in Software*, https://doi.org/10.1007/978-1-4842-6147-7_15

Own the room: Speak loudly, and stand up tall with a confident posture. Your audience will become bored if you send the message that you don't feel that you deserve to address them. Conversely, they will perk up if they feel that you are addressing them with vigor and passion.

Stick to three to five bullets per slide (usually): If you include much more, your audience will become overwhelmed reading. Of course, no rule is ironclad.

Never, ever read your slides verbatim: It's hard to think of something more painful than watching a speaker simply read the words off their slide. Presentations are opportunities to deliver energy, passion, and wit that you couldn't bring across on the printed page. Your slides should be minimal—enough that a reader can get the gist of your talk—but none of the flavor.

Interact with your audience: I find that asking questions of the audience and demanding answers are a good way to energize your viewers, because they get the pleasure of being challenged and becoming participants. You can ask a question with a surprising answer to open a section; you can have a quiz when you finish a section; you can warm up your talk by asking a (small) audience questions about themselves. This technique can be used a handful of times per talk.

Move fast: In an era when people can and will pull out their phones when they get bored, it's better to move too fast for your audience than too slow. Many people disagree with this advice, but I think it's far better to risk losing a small percentage of your audience than to let them fall asleep.

I hope and believe my last crumb of advice is *slightly* less facile than it seems: have fun. With practice, you'll find yourself getting in the zone and enjoying the spotlight, and your enjoyment will thaw your audience; you should enjoy your own jokes and look forward to a chance to connect with your audience and impress them. It takes time, but you can 100% get there—I have, and it certainly isn't where I started.

Technical Skills

The technical section of this book won't go deep on any specific technology or language, nor will it be a holistic introduction to software engineering. Instead, I'll try to highlight the highest-leverage principles of coding, debugging, operations, and software design that I haven't seen well taught elsewhere; my emphasis will be what I consider important in practice in industry. I'll also share a large list of specific practical tools I think every software engineer should learn about, including the usages you should focus on. My goal is to help you focus some of your applied study for the best possible practical returns. While I'm a backend and kernel engineer by training, I've attempted to keep this section general to all specialities.

Professional-Grade Code

This chapter evangelizes my personal favorite principles of code quality. It's neither an introduction to coding nor a comprehensive guide to writing good code but instead a small set of selected subjects I consider relevant to engineers adapting their academic skills to professional software. I'll note that a couple of these points (like "Don't Check Conditions that Your Codebase Precludes") may be controversial; if your team fervently rejects them, you can do your best to persuade, but remember that "You Can't Change Everything on Your First Day" (Chapter 9) and you should, when in doubt, Match The Codebase.

Master Language Conventions

The first step to writing good code is knowing your language backward and forward. I never start coding in a new language without reading a whole book about it (really) and reading whatever online style guides I can find. Small slipups are inevitable when you're getting started, but poor adherence to language conventions is easy to avoid, so it comes off as amateurish to experienced engineers. You can ask a colleague what sources they'd recommend for mastering your team's language(s).

© Daniel Heller 2020

D. Heller, *Building a Career in Software*, https://doi.org/10.1007/978-1-4842-6147-7_16

Naming

Most of our job turns out to be reading code as we try to find the perfect way to make changes to existing codebases; that includes reading our own code, which often feels like it was written by someone different and dumber than yourself.

The single best gift you can give future editors of your code, including yourself, is good function, type, and variable names. Comments and READMEs can become stale, and you usually have to jump around to consume them, but a crisp, explicit name often speaks for itself in-line; even if you still need richer documentation, a good name reduces the cognitive load of reading. Good naming has three objectives, in this order (according to me):

1. **Explicitness**: The name captures the role of the entity.

2. **Brevity**: The name is short and easy to read.

3. **Consistency**: The name follows the conventions of other similar entities in the codebase.

These objectives are in perpetual tension—the most explicit names often sacrifice some brevity, and the perfect name in isolation may stand out from other names in a codebase. You'll have to weigh all three, but my advice is to favor explicitness above all; try to save your readers the trouble of reading every line of a function to understand its meaning in a codebase. Once the name is explicit, make it as short as you can without loss of information. Here are a couple of examples of good and bad names I've seen in real life (or perpetrated):

Bad

```
// From the xnu (Mac OS X) kernel: "open1" is clearly a convenience for
// a programmer who can't think of a name that means something.
// How is it different from open()? Why does it exist?
int
open1(vfs_context_t ctx, struct nameidata *ndp, int uflags,
    struct vnode_attr *vap, fp_allocfn_t fp_zalloc, void *cra,
    int32_t *retval)
```

Not so bad

```
// Also from xnu; this function's name clearly indicates its relationship to
other functions—it is
// called with the lock already held.
vnode_t cache_lookup_locked(vnode_t dvp, struct componentname *cnp)
```

Match the Codebase

When writing code in an existing codebase, you should almost always match the coding conventions of that codebase even if you disagree with them; going off on your own will likely leave a confusing mess for future readers even if it does get past code reviewers, which it shouldn't. Some conventions—adding more comments, writing a better commit message, or naming more carefully—may be easy to integrate in a codebase incrementally but should always pass the smell test of "fitting in." Braces, spaces (as opposed to tabs), and compound_namingPatterns should never be changed unilaterally. If you think you should change the convention, remember that "You Can't Change Everything on Your First Day" (Chapter 9); be patient and stay humble when making your case.

Commenting

I'm sure you've heard the excellent advice to (a) comment liberally and (b) avoid comments that add no new information (like /* Merge merges */). Let me add a new principle: comments exist to help future readers (including yourself) gain a holistic sense of your code as quickly as possible. Therefore, like any good writer, you have the hard job of imagining the mindset of future readers and what they may not understand when they open YourStrangeDecisions.java. Here are four guidelines:

Motivation: The code is its own description of what it does and can be, if necessary, read in every detail to figure out its behavior. The motivation for your decision lives only in your own mind unless you write it down. and you can be certain that future readers will be curious.

```
// PageCache is a simple in-memory cache that can populate the
// homepage in the rare event that the recommender engine is down.
// It provides a slightly stale, incomplete, but extremely simple and
// highly available view of the homepage to ensure that we can
// always serve *something*. We have intentionally accepted a larger
// window of potential staleness to reduce the load on the DB.
```

Design: The reader's eyes can only see one piece of code at a time, and bootstrapping a grasp of the overall design through that peephole is really tough. Give the reader a hand.

```
// A refresher job repopulates the cache once per hour; see
// github.com/somecompany/cacherefresher. A "new-user" view of the page is
    synced
// into each frontend container and periodically reloaded from disk.
```

Assumptions or invariants: If a function or component has preconditions for correct behavior, even if asserted at runtime, they're good candidates for commenting; your colleague's shouldn't have to run their code and fail to learn your requirements.

Examples

```
// Until Status() returns success, all other APIs will return errors.
// _lookup must be called with the lock already held
```

Non-example (too obvious to need commenting):

```
// Save() only succeeds if the Database is available
```

Anything else nonobvious a reader might wonder about: "Nonobviousness" is slippery and very much in the eye of the beholder, but to the best of your ability, any nonobvious behaviors of a piece of code should be commented. Examples:

```
// Close() must be called when done or the connection will be leaked
// fetch() may fall back to a local cache if the DB is unavailable
```

Commit Messages Are Underrated

I've recently seen a trend to extremely brief, unhelpful commit messages like `Fix bug` or `Changes for my feature you've never heard of`. That's a problem; codebases evolve constantly, and in the limit, a codebase is its own documentation of what it does, but a year down the road, it can be hard or impossible to answer the perennial question: Why? Or, to put it differently, what the hey-hoo were those engineers thinking? A commit message is our one chance to capture our goals, design, and trade-offs at the time of our work for eternal posterity, even if the code later changes. Therefore, let's do better for our future selves and teammates. I suggest the following template:

```
<One-sentence summary of purpose>
<Blank line>
<Detailed explanation of purpose> <Design> <Tradeoffs, quirks, caveats>
```

Here's an example I dug up from the history of Git itself. Note that it includes the initial motivation, caveats, and thoughts for the future—you instantly get a sense of the point in time this commit messages represents in the evolution of the Git version control system.

```
commit bfe19f876cb20bea606e1a698030c017f31965c1
Author: Linus Torvalds <torvalds@osdl.org>
Date:   Sat Aug 6 18:01:03 2005 -0700
```

```
[PATCH] Extend "git reset" to take a reset point
```

This was triggered by a query by Sam Ravnborg, and extends "git reset" to reset the index and the .git/HEAD pointer to an arbitrarily named point.

For example

```
        git reset HEAD^
```

will just reset the current HEAD to its own parent - leaving the working directory untouched, but effectively un-doing the top-most commit. You might want to do this if you realize after you committed that you made a mistake that you want to fix up: reset your HEAD back to its previous state, fix up the working directory and re-do the commit.

If you want to totally un-do the commit (and reset your working directory to that point too), you'd first use "git reset HEAD^" to reset to the parent, and then do a "git checkout -f" to reset the working directory state to that point in time too.

```
Signed-off-by: Linus Torvalds <torvalds@osdl.org>
Signed-off-by: Junio C Hamano <junkio@cox.net>
```

Quick aside: Shouldn't we hear more discussion of how astonishing it is that Linus started Linux and Git?

Testing

I won't cover the subject of good testing in detail here; it's a profound and highly technical subject. I will offer a few simple principles:

- Code isn't high quality without tests, whatever the form your team may favor (unit, integration, end to end).

- If in doubt, start with true unit tests (i.e., tests that examine a single subcomponent in isolation, like a function, package, or class)—there's a special joy in refactoring a component with confidence because your unit tests cover its interface perfectly.

- You should measure code coverage, that is, what lines and branches of your program are exercised by your tests.

- There's no magic number for code coverage, but I prefer 100% when at all possible—the exceptions are usually libraries that make it hard to inject failure. If every line tested automatically, you can sleep much easier.

Cleverness

I'm opposed to it. Favor explicitness and simplicity over-cleverness whenever possible. If you can't avoid being clever, document it prodigiously. So, if you see some neat bitwise math that might get your calculation done in one line, or a neat pattern in a Haskell blog post you think you can emulate in Java, think twice or more; if you absolutely can't contain yourself, you had better add a comment explaining exactly where your life went off the rails.

Duplication vs. Reuse

Code reuse, and pushing ourselves to design carefully for reuse, is perhaps the single most-quoted principle of software design, and rightly so. I want to call out just one caveat to that principle: it can sometimes exist in tension with risk in production systems. Judiciously repeating yourself is underrated; as far as you are in this book, you can probably already tell that I think that. Generalizing a shared codepath can sometimes be higher risk than creating a new, similar function. Good tests reduce that risk. Your first impulse should always be toward reuse, but if it's difficult, if your confidence in tests is poor, and if the codepath is critical, you might consider duplicating.

Don't Check Nonsensical Conditions

If a function in your codebase requires a non-null argument and receives all its input from trusted functions, don't check for null. How to treat NULL, nil, or None depends on context—some types of code, like logging libraries, can make their users' lives easier by smoothly handling null-like arguments, and code that takes external input (e.g., over the wire) always needs to be ready for anything. However, internal routines that protect against nonsensical input encourage sloppy coding and confuse the reader—we should hold our own codebase to a higher standard. For example, the following cache should not check for nil; the callers should never let a nil get that far.

```
func (c *EntityCache) SaveUser(u *entities.User) error {
    ...
}
```

Open Source Conservatism

In 2018, a widely used open source Node.js package was accidentally handed off to a malicious new maintainer who surreptitiously injected code to steal cryptocurrency. The takeaway: taking on an open source dependency is not much different from installing and frequently running a program written by some rando on the Internet. That program may be very useful and worth the risk of malice, but try to think twice before you casually add new dependencies; if it only has one GitHub star, you should pass.

Tests Should Be Fast (Never Sleep)

A slow test is an infuriating obstacle to development velocity. Therefore, your tests should be fast. It's often tempting to sleep waiting for a condition like a timeout to occur (I've been guilty of this in my impetuous youth, but those sleeps can quickly add up to a painfully slow test suite). You can do better by injecting a clock interface everywhere, so you can mock that clock and accelerate time for tests. If you find your test suite taking more than a minute or two of every iteration on a diff, you should consider putting time into optimizing it; can you parallelize? Can you speed up setup?

Unit vs. Integration Testing

Integration tests can be slow; unit tests can be incomplete. A healthy test suite should have both; unit tests let us iterate quickly on changes in a component, shaping our work with frequent testing. Integration tests run longer but give us a higher degree of confidence that a component works with adjacent systems (which are no longer just mocked) before we send it to customers. My experience is that without unit tests, iteration becomes intolerably slow (see "Tests Should Be Fast"), but without integration tests, our confidence is unacceptably low before a system goes to production. Use both! I'd say that if you can absolutely only afford one, I'd prefer the confidence of an integration test, but it's a judgment call.

Inject Dependencies

Dependency injection is a coding convention of providing components their dependencies at the time they're created, rather than having a component instantiate its own dependencies. For example:

```
class ClassWithoutInjection {
    private IDBConnection dbConn;

    public ClassWithoutInjection() {
        this.dbConn = new DBConnection();
    }
}
```

```
class ClassWithInjection {
    private IDBConnection dbConn;

    public ClassWithInjection(IDBConnection dbConn) {
        this.dbConn = dbConn;
    }
}
```

Dependency injection's aim is to decouple components, making it easy to change the implementation of a dependency. Most importantly, if we inject an interface, we can swap in a mocked implementation, which is a lifesaver for testing, but we can equally swap in a wrapped object or, for example, a different database backend. You'll find countless DI frameworks on GitHub, and I'm not going to recommend one here. Suffice to say that I always favor the simpler, less magical, lighter-on-reflection ones.

Performance Last or a List of Priorities for Your Code

When I worked on the iOS kernel, I once reviewed a framework change where an engineer had researched my syscall interface and inserted the special trap instructions in our own code. Why?!, I asked, blind with rage—this handwritten assembly, inscrutable to the reader, would become an immensely hard-to-track-down bug if we ever changed our interface. His answer was performance, based on a superstitious theory of branch prediction. He was a smart and motivated engineer, but I felt then and feel now that this was profoundly misguided. I think our default priorities for a codebase should be

1. **Correctness**: The code does what it's supposed to do and is easy to verify (i.e., test).

2. **Maintainability**: The code is simple, easy for ourselves and others to change, and is likely to work under reasonable changes in operating conditions.

3. **Cost of development**: The code is fast to write, that is, minimizes engineering costs.

4. **Performance**: The code runs fast.

This is a simplification, because different systems have different priorities and sufficiently poor performance will break your system (no result is correct if the user gives up before they see it); you'll always have to weigh the Big Four priorities in context. However, it's a decent guideline to start your analysis.

In most systems, subtle, brilliant micro-optimizations buy a tiny grain of performance at a steep cost in maintainability and robustness, while network roundtrips and database calls limit the user-observed latency; we should only pay readability for performance when (a) performance really matters and (b) we have data to suggest that the specific optimization in question will help. Some codebases really do require ultrafast performance, like the inner loops in graphics and machine learning systems. In those rare cases, once you've measured and confirmed where the time is going, use every unreadable trick you have to make the code lightning fast.

Code Review

Code review is a standard industry practice where all production code changes are read by one or more other engineers to verify their correctness and quality. The practice is intended to prevent breakages and sustain the quality of codebases over time, and it's usually considered an important part of an engineer's duties. It's a partnership between two engineers; the author and the reviewer iterate together to produce the best change they can, meaning not just the best code quality but the best balance of code quality, testing, simplicity, and speed specific to the exact situation. It usually proceeds in cycles, with the reviewer asking questions and making suggestions, then the author answering those questions, accepting some suggestions, and pushing back on others. You're going to give and get tons of code reviews; this section will offer tips for how to do both effectively.

Receiving Code Reviews

I don't know of any science about the effectiveness of code review; you'll hear plenty about how it's cheaper to catch bugs in development than in production (which is true), but it also costs a lot of time; I don't think anyone truly knows whether it has positive returns. Nevertheless, as a neurotic, reliability-focused engineer, I love it. Every code review I receive is a gift from a colleague, and every bug they catch turns the grim embarrassment of an outage into the tiny embarrassment of an update to a diff.

You should strive for the same attitude; remember that when a reviewer finds a bug, it might slow you down today but not half as much as writing a postmortem would, and when they help you fix your style, they save you the contempt of future readers.

Therefore, you should seek out the toughest code reviewers you can, take their feedback seriously, and thank them for their help. When you receive feedback, every single comment should be addressed, and your default position should be to accept every comment unless you have a good reason not to. You absolutely can push back on feedback with good reason; you might feel that a suggestion is the wrong balance of simplicity vs. comprehensiveness, that it should best be handled in a separate change, or that it's simply wrong, and you can say those things. If you do, it should be gently and gratefully, with consideration for the reviewer's generosity in helping you. You should never ignore any comment; even if you choose not to act on it, you should acknowledge it. Because many questions may be subtle or debatable, you're welcome and encouraged to ask follow-up questions on feedback—does the reviewer feel strongly about that suggestion? Do they think it's okay to defer some changes for later? Why do they think that using this pattern is better than the other? You should strive to deeply understand their feedback and learn, not just rotely do what they say.

Reviewing Code

Giving a code review is partnering with a colleague to help them produce the best code they can for the situation. They send you the diff; you exhaustively scrutinize the code as you would your own; you ask questions and give suggestions; your partner answers your questions, tweaks their code, pushes back on some suggestions, and sends it back to you; you rinse and repeat until you agree the code is ready for prime time.

A great code review flows from domain knowledge and strong opinions about code quality; nothing I can tell you can substitute for mastery of a system and programming language. However, masters or not, review we must, and below are the questions I ask myself about any diff:

1. **Is it correct?** This is obviously the primary question. To evaluate correctness, you must first understand exactly what a change is intended to do; if you're not sure, you're not ready to review (and the commit message probably leaves something to be desired!). Second, you must understand the system—do the functions return what this code expects them to? Is that really the right port? Those are things you should check, not assume. Finally, it requires you to read in detail, checking edge cases, error handling, threading, language usage, etc., etc., etc.

2. **Is it clear?** For me, this is foremost about naming, commenting, and simplicity, in that order, but can also bear on function length, commit messages, file layout, and so on. I take a heavy hand when commenting about clarity, and you should too.

3. **Does it match the code around it?** This is related but not identical to clarity; you should enforce consistency. Code style is the first consideration here, but quality trade-offs can also be matched of flouted. For example, it might (or might not) come off as silly to demand polish in an ad hoc test script; looking at the existing conventions is the only way to fine-tune your feedback.

4. **Does it reinvent anything?** Duplication isn't always bad, but you should prima facie expect reuse, and duplication should be explained. Is there already a function they could use for some of the new code? Could they reuse an existing tool?

5. **Is it well-tested?** This more or less speaks for itself. Again, you need to weigh this in light of the existing conventions—demanding 100% coverage may be out of place in some teams/systems. However, you should err toward asking for full coverage.

6. **Is it idiomatic?** This question can only be answered by mastering your team's languages yourself, which you must do.

7. **Is the diff reasonably sized?** Large diffs are hard to review and hard to get right; though not always avoidable, you should discourage them and look for smaller atoms that could be delivered separately.

The biggest question you'll likely have to ask yourself as you start a review is: How deep should I go? If you're a master of the code they're editing, you're in luck, but usually, you'll need to make some decisions about what to trust and what to verify (like, "what exactly are the semantics of that value of the state enum?"). My advice is to go deep; answering questions for yourself is a great way to learn codebase, and the extra scrutiny will (often) be appreciated. As always, judge in context, and ask for advice to find your way to the right balance.

Beyond the Code

There are a few key considerations beyond how you read the actual code.

First is the tone of feedback. Code review feedback should always be supportive; we err toward trusting our colleagues' diligence. You should never try to score points or let contempt creep into your feedback; you're helping a friend. Softeners like "I think" and "what do you think?" may seem superfluous, but they can make all the difference; "This is bad style; it should be snake_case" will put people on edge compared to "I don't think this is idiomatic Python; snake_case is preferred according to the style guide." If that seems contrived, trust me that you'll hear both tones all the time.

Second is latency. You'll discover quickly that long waits for code reviews are incredibly frustrating, especially when collaborating across time zones. Save your colleague that frustration by treating code reviews as top-priority tasks, preempting any nonurgent work (unless you're so deep in something that switching is very costly).

Third, I'll advise against a common antipattern: the ping-pong review pair. Two people shouldn't constantly review each other's code without anyone else getting a look, because a pair system like that can easily devolve into rubber-stamping at low quality. You should try to get some diversity of perspective in the code review stream for every area.[1]

Finally, there's the question of when to hold the line on quality and when to bend. Remember that this is contextual, not absolute; some code really doesn't need to be great. If your team doesn't philosophically value code quality the way you do, remember that you can't change everything on the first day; you should try to level the team up gradually and respectfully (never throwing a fit). When it comes to incorrectness, I'll usually draw a hard line. For a codebase I own or wrote from scratch, I also feel empowered to demand that code meets my standards. For common code, especially when you're junior to your colleagues, you can aim for epsilon above the median—inch in the right direction, but accept that conventions take time to change.

---

[1] You can consider bending this rule for efficiency when you're an experienced engineer working with other experienced engineers, but that's years away!

Debugging

This chapter aims to set you on a path to becoming an effective professional debugger. It starts with a discussion of how to think about debugging—as a search problem where we aim to improve our understanding of a problem as efficiently as possible. Then, I'll offer a menu of approaches for different kinds of problems. Since debugging often draws on pattern matching against years of experience, this chapter is just a start, but I hope it accelerates your learning.

The Philosophy of Debugging

Debugging is a search problem. We have a system which is 99.999% correct (or it wouldn't work at all), but somewhere deep in its implementation or environment, one of a million things is rotten. We debug in a loop of hypothesizing and experimenting, gradually refining a mental model of the system until only that one in a million explanations remains:

1. Mentally model system; hypothesize what's wrong if you can.[1]

2. Imagine what data would most precisely confirm, disprove, or refine our theory.

3. Get that data.

---

[1]Sometimes we can't start with a hypothesis precise enough to be interesting. In that case, we still go get the data we think are most likely to improve our understanding.

© Daniel Heller 2020
D. Heller, *Building a Career in Software*, https://doi.org/10.1007/978-1-4842-6147-7_17

4. Confirm, reject, or refine the model.

5. Go to 1.

Effective debugging means getting answers as quickly as we can, not by typing faster but by choosing the best data to collect and drawing the most precise conclusions from those data; minimizing our total search time with smart heuristics for which data will be most informative and disciplined interpretations of that data.

This all may seem too abstract; don't worry. I think it'll start to make sense in time, but here's a more concrete framing.

Effective debugging is always collecting information to point the finger at the cause of a problem—good debuggers know the biggest variety of data to collect and make the best choices about what to collect based on what they already know. For example, suppose we are seeing frequent latency spikes in our API calls.

Step	Hypothesis	Why	Data Collection	Result
1	Some back-end service is stuttering	Experience; more likely service than network or other Byzantine problem	Look at distributed tracing graph for slow request; it can tell us which service has a problem	Yes, looks like it's extra time in the product data service
2	Database might be slow	Experience; this is a common cause of latency	Look at database query latency graphs; it can tell us quickly whether the database is indeed at fault, so we can dig in there	Database query performance seems steady; this hypothesis is wrong
3	Second-best guess: it might be garbage collection in the service	Experience; GC is another common type of slowdown	Look at JVM GC time graphs (from JMX data); they can tell us quickly whether we're seeing GC activity	Yes, service is having major garbage collection
4	There might be excessive allocation of some type of object	Experience; pressure is probably caused by one to two object types	Run jmap; look for suspiciously high counts; it can quickly point out a bad allocation pattern	Seems like heap is filled with entries for what should be a pretty small cache
5	The cache size might not set properly	We know our service: this cache should be small	Check the code; cache misconfiguration can be easily spot-checked	Cache size is too large, debugging done

At each stage, we start with our best guess of what could be going wrong given our current knowledge, then choose data to collect that we think might efficiently help us accept or reject that possibility. While we're always hypothesis-driven, when we start investigating a problem with minimal data, our "hypothesis" might be extremely broad, even so broad as to basically be, I'll check the richest data source—"it might be something I can see in the logs."

Just Do Something, or "Debugging is Hard, Though"

"Just Do Something" (Chapter 5) discusses how a bias to action is the mother of effectiveness; debugging is where we put that into practice most of all. In the most orderly debugging processes, we steadily refine our hypothesis by collecting data of intuitive value. If it were always that easy, they wouldn't pay us the big bucks. Many problems defy simple analysis—the failures are weird and complicated, none of the usual suspects apply, or the failure just involves technology we don't know well. That doesn't need to stop you—when others would stop, do something. The next section will offer a menu of debugging techniques, the all-stars that you can trot out even when the available data don't offer a clear path—ways we can "go fishing" for clues. At some point, you may exhaust even these, at which point you'll ask for help (see Chapter 14) as precisely and respectfully as possible,[2] but there's plenty to try first.

Debugging Menu

This section offers an all-star team of things to try when you're debugging, ordered very roughly from most to least likely to help you solve a problem. Its goal is to help you remember (a) what your options are and (b) that you're seldom really stuck when you take on your first few real-world problems.

1. **Logs**: A log is a (usually) human-readable string printed somewhere a human can find it—syslog, systemd journal, Splunk, Kibana, /var/log, docker logs, database logs (especially slow query logs), kubectl logs, whatever you've got. When something goes wrong, checking error logs is almost always one of the most powerful options, because most systems produce logs when things go wrong (and even when they go right). Don't see anything at first

---

[2] Note that you'll tend to ask for help much faster during production outages, when time is of the essence.

glance? Don't know what log to look for? Don't give up! Do a wildcard search for something related to your problem. Don't see anything? Try a few more related terms. Try filtering/aggregating by process name, service name, hostname, screen, username, entity ID, time, or any other property at all that you think might be associated with the problem.

2. **Metrics**: A metric is basically a tiny little log designed for aggregation—a number with identifying keys, supporting aggregation to describe counts, latencies, and rates like on-disk bytes, response time, and error rate. Where logs usually describe a single event, metrics usually describe a system's aggregate behavior, and metrics will usually capture general systemic degradation. You don't need to know exactly what metric to look for or what dashboard to check—you can usually search for service dashboards by name in your metrics front end, and once you have a relevant dashboard in your browser, you can usually search for the right graph by name or just look for any line that seems to have gone up or down recently.

3. **Chrome dev tools**: Whether your problem is UI misbehavior, failing requests to the back end, or weird data, Chrome offers a rich view of the interaction between a page and the back end; you can at least crack open the Network tab and look at what's being requested and returned for all XHRs before you give up!

4. **Just grep the code**: If you've seen an error message you don't understand or even a behavior whose name you can guess, just go search for it! I've found time and again that I can solve problems others don't because I'm willing to take an educated guess and search for it.

5. **Add new instrumentation**: Don't have the logs or metric you really need? Add them, whether on your laptop, in staging, or in a production environment.

6. **Local system monitors**: Tools like top, htop, iotop, and iostat tell you about CPU, memory, and disk consumption in real time. If you think something funky might be happening on a computer (e.g., your process might be starved for CPU or I/O), a quick look at these tools can shine a light.

7. **git bisect**: If you think a change in git broke something, a binary search across commits can point the finger without your needing to understand the problem at all— just check out one commit at a time, and test it until you find the earliest broken one.

8. **Debugger**: Debuggers like GDB offer you the deepest possible introspection of a running process, including printing variables, stepping through functions, and scripting data structure traversals. Their learning curves are often steep, and they may be unreliable under some conditions, but when you need to understand a mysterious crash, these are by far the most powerful tools.

9. **CPU profiler**: A view of where a program spends its CPU cycles over time is often the best way to understand performance problems and even some crashes. Tooling varies across languages, but good examples include Linux perf, the built-in Go profiler, Java's VisualVM (or even jstack), and Mac OS X's sample.

10. **Heap introspection**: Similarly, for memory leaks, a heap profile is indispensable; look for language-specific tools like jmap and Go's heap profiler.

11. **tcpdump/ngrep/wireshark**: These incredibly powerful tools can show you what's really going on on the wire, so anytime you suspect problems with TCP interactions, encoding issues, or just want to see what's really going on on the network, start here. Note that TLS makes things more difficult (though not impossible).

12. **Tracing frameworks**: Often the richest examination of a program's behavior over time can come from tools that can aggregate a variety of events over time; these include Linux's strace (system call tracing; the easiest to use and most frequently helpful of these), Linux perf (it can do more than CPU profiling), or the wildly powerful DTrace. Apart from strace, these are power tools with steep learning curves.

Running Experiments

Software engineers are seldom subject to anything like the rigorous research integrity demands of physical science or medicine, because most of our experiments are (a) for our own use (not intended for publication) and (b) don't involve human subjects in the same sense as a medical study. Nevertheless, we do run experiments, often to debug problems, measure system performance, or choose between customer experiences. When we do, we can save confusion and frustration for ourselves and others by adopting a "lab notebook" style of carefully recording our actions as we take them in a raw, durable log that can be trusted after the fact.

My own experience early in my career was that when I was running more complex multistage experiments, I was apt to get confused partway through and either fail to execute a key step, forget what I had/hadn't already done, or somehow fail to capture the result I cared about (e.g., clearing the screen before copying a result). That all may sound silly, but the steps to run an experiment can be quite complex—installing builds, restarting systems, changing configuration, hooking up external instruments, monitoring during the run, and finally collecting the right data at the end, all potentially under time pressure.[3]

My most painful experimentation process was around overload resilience, after a system I'd worked on experienced a cascading failure during an unexpected use surge. After a ton of work to harden the systems, we needed to run overload tests all the way to failure to ensure that the system could really get overloaded and continue to serve some users, rather than hitting the deck face first (see "Plan for Overload"). It wasn't possible to replicate our complicated production environment end to end in staging, and we could only secure two hours a week to run a full-scale test. That meant that those two hours were extremely critical, and if things went wrong, we had another week before we could finish the hardening project and, more importantly, satisfy ourselves that our system was robust. At least twice, we showed up unprepared—some part of the testing infrastructure wasn't ready, we didn't know which configuration changes needed to be made, we failed to collect the right data while we had the chance, etc.

We finished the test successfully in the end, and I want to recommend two methods that helped us get there.

- **Making a detailed runbook** (checklist) for the experiment, including setup, running, and data collection; during the experiment, verbally going through every step as a team. Then, when reviewing the checklist prior to execution, ensure that all dashboarding, data collection docs, etc. are prepared in advance.

- **Recording *everything* done during the experiment**, with screenshots, copy–pastes, and links in a single Google Doc; especially, time-stamping the completion of stages of the checklist.

---

[3]Time pressure occurs particularly when you're experimenting on a production system or shared singleton and only have a narrow maintenance window or reservation.

The runbook serves two purposes. First, it forces you to focus your thinking during the planning stage of the experiment so you minimize the risk of showing up for the experiment and not knowing what to do. That will probably still happen (it's hard to anticipate everything), but you'll at least have reduced the risk. Second, it organizes your progress during the event; it's harder to miss steps when you're reading a list out loud.

The "Lab Notebook" document, with time-stamped notes on every single thing we did, ensures that we always know after the fact exactly what happened; particularly, when the time comes to communicate our results, we can say with high confidence what happened when and what we saw; we'll never need to mumble and evade when asked what happened

Building for Reliability

This chapter is about reliability. It is again not a deep technical manual but instead encourages a mindset of frequently visualizing an uncertain future where you, your code, or your colleagues need to respond to changing conditions. That mindset is general, but we'll move on from there to list some of the most important areas for concern in building any reliable system.

Think About the Future

A reliability-focused approach to building software starts with constantly asking the question: **What could happen, and how will we be ready?** It's that exercise of imagining the future that lets us arm ourselves with the right preparation to keep a system running. To be more specific

- What could break?

- How can the system keep working if something breaks?

- What could fail without our realizing it? How can we make sure we'll be alerted?

- What might we be asked to (or want to) change in the future? Will it be easy?

© Daniel Heller 2020
D. Heller, *Building a Career in Software*, https://doi.org/10.1007/978-1-4842-6147-7_18

- What would I want to know if something breaks?
- What behavior would I want to be able to control or change if something goes wrong?
- What could users do that we don't intend?
- What could be inconvenient, slow, or error-prone when we have customer problem?
- What might trip up a future developer of the system?
- What precondition or required invariant isn't documented or tested?

This is at best an imperfect science of pattern matching and educated guesswork; you'll get more accurate and more precise as your knowledge grows, and you don't need to hold yourself to perfection. We all miss things and draw on the shared experience and wisdom of a team to achieve the best foresight. However, you can at least ask yourself the questions.

Design for Failure

System failures are inevitable—hard drives, RAM, switches, routers, and, above all, humans fail every single day. You already know to check your return values so you don't crash when your code encounters errors; don't stop doing that, but this principle says that you should look beyond the goal of "not crashing" to designs and implementations that (a) achieve unaltered or gently degraded user experiences even when things go wrong—online failure resilience—and (b) can be recovered when they experience disaster, support disaster recovery. The best reference I know of on these subjects is *Site Reliability Engineering: How Google Runs Production Systems*, and you should read it without delay, but I'm going to give you a little motivation here.

We'll group failure resilience techniques into two big categories:

Redundancy: The very best case in the presence of failure is to deliver an unaltered user experience. This is an extremely rich and complex subject mostly beyond the scope of this book, but its essential technique is redundancy—having more than one of something so that if one fails (e.g., a human puts bad code on it), another keeps working. We can then help the user out with either a resilient distributed algorithm (like ZooKeeper might use) or a retry.

Graceful degradation: Sometimes an unaltered experience is impossible—maybe you're writing mobile code, the request for user history failed, and we've already made the user wait as long as we can. Can we show an experience that's less rich but still sane? Can we do things like show an unpersonalized view of the product, use a heuristic instead of machine learning prediction, or serve from a local durable cache that may be stale but will be sane? Can we generally "fail open," doing *something* for the user despite failure? To make a decision, we need to reason deeply about which user experiences might be acceptable and which might not. If we've tried everything we can and there's no way to deliver a sane user experience, we should do our best to show a helpful and attractive error message; at the very least, we should offer the user, "Sorry, we're having a problem with our server, please try again in a few minutes"—don't ever let me catch you showing the user "Error 0xCADE1F."

Plan for Data Loss

Disaster recovery is the tooling for our worst nightmare: the loss of data or system state such that customer experiences may be down for days or indefinitely. Companies have failed for its lack; for motivation, I encourage you to try to visualize yourself and your beloved colleagues after an operator accidentally runs `drop table users` or cancels your GCP accounts or deletes your S3 buckets. The only route to safe harbor are the following:

Offline copies of your data, not just replicas: Data that can't be irrevocably corrupted by a single bad SQL command or code deploy. These backups are only as trustworthy as the last time you tested restoring them, so test often.

System state restorable from source control: If your system setup requires extensive imperative human tweaking, then if your system is hit by a meteor, you're in big, big trouble—it's almost guaranteed to be a colossal effort to turn it up, and your company will be failing while you're trying to restore it. *Everything* should be automatically restorable from git (or your source control of choice).

Build for Debugging (or Observability Is Everything)

Building observability into a system lets us ensure that (a) we can detect if it breaks and (b) when that happens, we have the tooling to figure out why.

Table stakes are metrics and logs aggregated in centralized databases, subjects given a satisfactory introduction in *Site Reliability Engineering*. When we're coding, we ask: What conditions will I want to detect, and what metrics will let me build that alerting? When a problem happens, what logs will I want to see? When I log that error message, what extra context will let me quickly see not just what broke but why? Examples include logging the ID of the entity you failed to fetch, the SQL query that failed to execute, or the error message you got from your IAAS provider; you'll do yourself a favor by investigating error wrapping, the practice of combining data from a low-level error with higher-level context. For example, the following would tell us both what our application was trying to do and what the underlying API provider thought about it:

```
uuid := itemInfo.UUID()
item, err := itemService.Metadata(uuid)
if err != nil {
    return errors.Wrapf(err, "item service failed to fetch item metadata for
    %s", uuid)
}
```

We don't need to stop there—many expert savvy engineers build simple, mostly static debugging UIs into their services, preparing for fast introspection of a single service instance under time pressure. I recently discovered that a colleague had built a simple little HTML UI into a long-running CLI tool, which is some next-level commitment to observability.

I personally feel that there's almost no software pleasure greater than hitting a problem and knowing that you already added the *perfect* log.

Build for Operator Intervention

Once we've detected a problem, we usually want to do something; we should write our code to support that emergency intervention when the time comes. That usually means building endpoints, dynamic configuration, or UI controls to rapidly change a system's behavior without building and deploying new code. For example, we could build in the ability to

- Improve scalability by reducing the maximum number of results we return.

- Fall back to an older, unsophisticated behavior (e.g., a heuristic instead of machine learning).

- Disable cache prefetching in case it for some reason runs amok and blows up the heap.

Build For Rollback

Most production problems are caused by human actions; therefore, our most potent remediation is usually to undo what humans did. That means that if at all possible, rollback should be fast and easy, and you should never, ever make a truly backward-incompatible change; it has ample "must-fix-forward" horror stories to set you on an honest path.

Ideally, code change rollouts should be quite easy to revert, with a blue-green deploy or easy way to reset the "running" version to a trusted build. New features, including backend, mobile, and web, are best deployed behind configuration control that allows them to be swiftly and orthogonally rolled back. Most importantly, database schema changes should be backward-compatible almost always (e.g., add a column, don't delete); we should run on the new schema for weeks before the old data are deleted.

Don't Order Dependencies; Wait

The best engineer I ever worked with taught me this principle in a random offhand comment; I've never been more reminded that the very best engineers don't just hack but generalize, finding the reusable principle they can share with everyone. He said, roughly: when building a system with a complex dependency graph, especially a distributed system, it's tempting to enforce an explicit startup ordering and fail hard if dependencies aren't available when we start. Unfortunately, this is hard to maintain (you'll always forget to specify one edge in the graph) and also brittle—if your dependency stutters, crashes, or is restarted, you may fail hard. Better it is to have each component calmly wait for its dependencies, retrying with some backoff; then you never need to maintain an explicit graph, and your system will tend to heal when the unexpected happens.

Plan for Overload

Even with good capacity planning, we may experience temporary request spikes beyond a system's capacity—for example, due to a promotion or an unexpected trip to the front page of Reddit. Those spikes may overwhelm the least scalable components of our systems and cause errors. An ideal system continues to serve the maximum possible number of requests successfully, failing only those in excess of capacity and recovering smoothly when load returns to normal. Many systems, though, fail completely: their success rates go to zero, and they may remain unavailable long after their workload returns to normal. Figure 18-1 illustrates these cases.

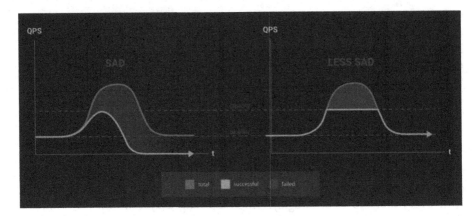

Figure 18-1. Leveling off under overload vs. failing

The most common reason for that prolonged downtime is excessive queueing. Most systems queue requests for processing with some pool of resources (e.g., threads or database connections). If request volume exceeds maximum throughput, those queues can become more and more full, sometimes to the point that a request will already be worthless (i.e., user has given up) when it reaches the head of the queue. In pathological cases, a system may spend many minutes, or even hours, draining queues of useless work after request volume returns to normal. I've worked on maybe ten serious outages caused by this kind of excessive queuing.

There exist well-known techniques, like the controlled delay algorithm, for counteracting this problem; many systems, particularly databases, do not implement them. The solutions to these problems are circuit breaking and adaptive load shedding (i.e., dropping excessive requests), which avoid filling queues when systems are already beyond their capacity. If we find ourselves in this scenario without the aid of those tools, restarting services and databases becomes the only game in town, so

- Bound your queue sizes; consider LIFO rather than FIFO!

- Use a circuit-breaking library any time you use a service client.

- Use an inbound loadshedder if you can! A CPU-based load-shedding trigger can be easy to configure.

- Ensure you have some way to rate-limit inbound traffic, whether at load balancers/forwarding plane or at the service level.

Data Layer Isolation (In Which Database Migrations Are Our Biggest Problem)

In Real Life™, it often feels like most engineering effort is spent migrating from one system to another—either from one database to another or one microservice to another. That means that one of the most painful common obstacles is data access code sprinkled together with business logic, like a SQL query embedded in your controller or data model; SQL queries, often being literally just string literals, are particularly hard to find and analyze when doing migrations. You'll do your future self a favor by reviewing the MVCS pattern; keep data access code like microservice requests and SQL queries in its own layer with as tight an interface as possible, hopefully enabling you to swap out databases and downstream services with less painful hunting, pecking, and refactoring.

Mastering the Command Line

This chapter is a guide to the command line tools you should learn for the biggest bang for the buck. Mastery of the command line is important for two reasons: first, because it can make you much faster in day-to-day tasks, even ones as simple as browsing code in a codebase and, second, because it's a way to signal to other programmers that you mean business. I wouldn't exactly call it a shibboleth—it's useful for reasons beyond helping programmers recognize our own—but good command line skills do build a little cred, and a little cred never hurt anyone.

This list is nowhere close to the end of what you should learn, but if you familiarize yourself with everything on the list, you'll be well on your way. Looking down the barrel of two pages of pages of bullets, that prospect probably seems daunting, but many of these tools are quite simple and can be learned in minutes. For each one, you should read the entire man page[1] where one exists; you won't retain everything, but you just might remember something when it counts. Where there's no man page, you can find a blog post or buy a book.

---

[1]Unix manual page; on the command line; try running man man to learn more.

© Daniel Heller 2020

D. Heller, *Building a Career in Software*, https://doi.org/10.1007/978-1-4842-6147-7_19

Shell

Command of your shell is the foundation for every other tool I'll mention. Bash is my shell of choice, and tldp.org has my favorite bash documentation, but there are countless good books and blog posts out there. If you prefer zsh, I won't stop you (and you might be on to something). If you prefer csh... well, it takes all kinds. Here's a minimal set of things to master.

- I/O redirection and pipes: These will allow you to rapidly build complex ad hoc tooling by composing other tools, which you'll have to do all the time. You should at the very least know >, >>, <, |, >&, and <<.

- cd: learn to back up with -.

- Backgrounding with &.

- Killing and suspending with ctrl-c and ctrl-z; foregrounding with fg.

- Setting and reading variables; quoting and escaping therein.

- Special variables: $?, !$, !!, $#, %%, $!, $_, $0 through $9 (command line arguments).

- Configuring your environment:

  - PATH, .bashrc, and .bash_profile

  - Aliases

- for and while loops: I write ad hoc loops to iterate over static or dynamic lists literally every day.

- read into a variable (often in a while loop).

- if-then-else, [[ ]]; file and string tests like -z, -n, and their many friends.

- Helpful shell config settings like (in bash) set -x, set -e, set -u, set -o pipefail.

- Up arrow and ctrl-r for browsing history.

- hash -r and hash -d for managing cached paths to tools.

- Defining functions.

- Environment variables.

- PIPESTATUS.

- `which`: see where a command comes from.
- `/dev/null`.
- String substitutions and default values: `${foo:-bar}`, `${foo:=bar}`, `${foo#bar}`, and many more.

Information Discovery and Text Manipulation

When I'm debugging a really tough problem, I often reflect that it seems to demand every Unix skill I have, but top among them is teasing a story out of code or logs without knowing what files matter, what format they're written in, what's normal or abnormal, etc. Even when I enjoy the benefit of an IDE or an aggregation system, I often end up falling back on the precision and composability of Unix commands; `find` with wildcards to hunt for logs and config files that seem relevant; `grep` for `fail` or `error` or some relevant term; `sort` and `uniq` and `wc -l` to figure out what's happening often or rarely. The software world runs on text, and you should be fast and smooth at figuring out what it says.

- `grep`: The original search tool. Emphasis on `-R`, `-l`, `-L`, `-E` (with | for "or"), and `-v`.
- `find`: Identify files, including complex boolean tests.
- `xargs`: For turning output of one command into arguments to the next; often a better option than a while loop.
- `ls`: Get familiar with at least `-R`, `-d`, `-t`, `-l`, `-1`.
- `cat`: Extract file content.
- `sort` and `uniq`; when ad hoc debugging, almost nothing is more useful than `<do something> | sort | uniq -c` # How many of each type?
- `awk`: at least enough to print columns (it's extremely rich, but column printing is a great start): `awk '{print $1}'`:
  - You can also try cut, but I prefer awk.
- `wc`: How many words, characters, or lines in a body of text? `my-tool | sort | uniq | wc`.
- `less`, `head`, and `tail` for quick glances a files.
- `sed`: Complex and powerful, but you should learn enough for simple substring replacement.

- Regular expressions: Learn the basics; they pay off again and again.

- column: Align text into columns.

- tr: fast character mappings.

Special Section for the Best Tool Ever

I've never met an engineer familiar with jq who doesn't consider it a remarkable achievement; some say, including me, that it may be the greatest tool ever written—a one-stop shop for processing json. You should spend a cozy afternoon with the man page; try to go beyond the basic usage.

Networking

These tools are extremely deep, and you don't need to understand everything. Reading the man pages and experimenting with the basic usages will serve you well; whether you work on mobile, back end, frontend, or embedded systems, you are guaranteed to eventually want to know what a network is doing:

- ping: confirm you can reach a host/IP.

- dig and host: DNS.

- netstat: List sockets on your host. If nothing else, remember netstat -nap.

- curl and its countless options for ad-hoc HTTP requests. If nothing else, you should be able to pass headers and change your HTTP verb without looking at the man page.

- nc: Ad hoc TCP (like sending some bytes over a TCP connection).

- To examine a host's IP networking: ifconfig on mac, ip on Linux.

Local and Remote Sessions

This section may be more relevant to backend engineers than to frontend and mobile hackers, but if you're one of the former, then it's for certain that you need to deal with computers other than the one you're typing on.

- ssh: Tunnel with -L and -R, and glance at the -o options. Learn to run both interactive sessions and one-shot commands.

- scp and rsync for copying files across machines (rsync is your friend when performance becomes a bottleneck).
- tmux or screen: Multiple shells in a single window and sessions you can rejoin on remote machines.[2]

Running Processes and Host State

On production systems and on your own laptop, it's often (daily) handy to ask: What's running? What's it doing? Is the host healthy? When did this process fail?

- ps, pgrep, top, pstree, and htop for looking at running processes
- lsof for looking at open files
- pkill, kill, and killall for sending signals
- iostat/iotop for I/O behavior
- df and du for disk usage
- journalctl and systemctl for logs and daemon state on Linux
- strace for observing system calls on Linux
- /proc for more process details on Linux

Databases

You should master the command line of whatever database you're using; I promise that you will need to introspect the DB at some point and that this will be the best way.

Git

You are almost certainly going to work with Git, and you should be great at it—it is guaranteed to pay off. I suggest getting comfortable with the following; it wouldn't kill you to read the whole man page for each.

- git cherry-pick
- git rebase (favor this over merging! It will make your histories cleaner)

---

[2]To my eternal shame, I haven't mastered either; I believe I'll start a sprint on tmux this week.

- `git log`
- `git shortlog`
- `git tag`
- `git show`
- `git reset` and `git reset --hard`
- `git stash`
- `git status`
- `git rev-parse`

Miscellany

I've tried to come up with a clever theme to unify the tips below; even though I've failed on that account, you should learn them:

- The ISO8601 standard for dates: You don't need to pass around times as Unix timestamps or with ambiguous day–month ordering. Use a standard! Ref: `date --iso-8601`.

- `md5` and `sha1sum` for when you need a quick checksum, especially when you want to check if two files are the same without sending their bytes over the wire!

- `uuidgen -v4` for when you need a random UUID.

- If you use a Mac:

  - `pbcopy` and `pbpaste` for using the Mac clipboard in shell pipelines.

  - `open` for opening browser windows (or other apps) from the shell.

  - homebrew (`brew`) for package management.

- `autojump` is one of the best tips I've ever gotten, for faster command line navigation; look it up.

Operating Real Software

Perhaps the most important difference between academic software and professional software is that the latter must be operated—once it works, it needs to keep working (or, return to working) across hardware failures, operator errors, bad deploys, and changes in usage. Fifteen years ago, it was all but guaranteed that an engineer would write their code and hand it off to an intrepid operations (ops) engineer for the hard job of keeping things working; while that model still exists, every day the industry moves more towards having the engineers who write software own its operation.

I'm unreservedly in favor of this model, because (a) authors have the deepest expertise in their own systems and (b) it's healthy for engineers to bear the responsibility, and the strong incentives of getting paged for our own bad code.

Operating software, however, demands different skills and practices than writing it; built on good design for operators, in the moment it depends on discipline, fast decision-making, and an extreme sense of responsibility and ownership. This chapter is a brief introduction to safe production practices, on call, and outages; it aims to prepare you to join a professional software team as a high-functioning, responsible operator.

© Daniel Heller 2020
D. Heller, *Building a Career in Software*, https://doi.org/10.1007/978-1-4842-6147-7_20

Respect Production

I posit: production systems run real stuff, and real people rely on them; when they break, people's days, investments, and careers are wrecked. Further: the biggest threat to production systems is software engineers. The vast majority of outages, in my experience, are caused by human mistakes, and even conceptually correct perturbations can break things (maybe the deployment system itself is causing problems!).

Therefore, you should take production very, very seriously—for most engineers, your job, above all else, is to keep it working.

You should be sweating with fear when you change production (I promise you, I am!), and you should only ever do so when armed with a deep understanding of what you're doing. If you're in a shred of doubt about whether a change is safe, you should refrain unless an emergency demands it—it's far better to ask a dumb question than break a critical system.

When things do (inevitably) go wrong, your best insurance policy is the expertise and alertness of experienced operators. That means that deploying, releasing, or changing configuration when those other experts are online is safe-ish; deploying when you're alone and they're off drinking or sleeping in their comfy, comfy beds is dangerous. Ergo: don't deploy on Friday afternoon, don't deploy on the weekend, and don't deploy at night; above all, never, ever deploy and walk away,[1] because as the initiator you're the person most able to help if things go wrong.

On Call

"On Call" in software is responsibility for rapidly fixing software systems when they break. It usually means a 1-day or 1-week shift where some problem-reporting system (a phone number, app, or literal pager) is routed to you and you commit to responding quickly to address problems that threaten your company's customers—and therefore business. This chapter will discuss the theory and practice of being on call—why the role exists, what it means to a company, and the basic principles that will apply to almost any specific on-call job you may have. Before we get into the theory, here's an example to give you the flavor of it.

---

[1] Or get on a plane, or on a boat, or anywhere you might not be reachable! Sketchy plane WiFi does not count as reachability!

A Basic Example

Here's the most canonical example of an on-call incident I can think of: you get a push notification in your PagerDuty mobile app that the rate of errors for requests to your site's home page is higher than expected—5%. You log into your dashboards and confirm that the error rate is 5%, where it was under 1% five minutes ago. You find that someone has just made a configuration change to the site. You announce what you've found in your team's Slack room, then roll back the change (return the system to its previous state), and the error rate returns to normal.

Why We Care

Software on call resembles in many respects on-call duties in other domains subject to sudden crises, such as medicine. The on-call person is the tactical owner of problems as they happen in real time, ensuring that problems never fall through the cracks—that there is someone responsible (and accountable) for organizing a prompt, sensible response for the organization.

This role can be of existential importance—issues like data corruption can cause irreparable damage to a company's reputation. A friend of a friend of mine actually worked at a company that literally shut down after a data loss incident! Therefore, though it is usually only a small part of the responsibilities of a software engineer, it demands special attention.

Five Principles

Jobs, systems, and on-call duties differ greatly one to the next; nevertheless, certain principles apply in nearly every case, and if you keep them in mind, you can improvise when domain knowledge fails you. Here are my personal five foundational principles of on-call.

Protect the customer: This is the ultimate purpose of being on-call, and when in doubt, you should ask yourself, what does the most to protect the customer right now?

Always pick up the phone (or respond to the page, or the chat, etc., etc.): Your job is to make sure someone responds, and if you don't, no one will! *Not* picking up the phone is an appalling, in some cases fireable, lapse in responsibility.

Ensure chain of custody: *Someone* must always be driving a problem; that might not be you, but if it comes to you first, your part isn't done until you are 100% sure that someone else is owning it (and knows that they're owning it). I prefer to hear the new owner say, "yes, I will own this problem."

Focus on mitigation: Your goal is to return systems to good health; deep understanding can wait and is very possibly a distraction (e.g., you shouldn't care one bit what about a bad change broke the site; if the change was bad, you should roll it back and ask questions later).

Don't give up: If you don't know what to do, try something; if you can't think of anything, escalate (call someone else) without hesitation. Always keep pushing toward resolution. I've called colleagues at 3 AM to protect customers more than once, and I wouldn't hesitate to do it again.

Just Roll Back

If you have only one tool as an on-call engineer, rollback should be it. Most production problems are due to human changes; therefore, the foremost tool of the production operator is undoing human changes. We should use that tool extremely liberally, because it's safe (at least for services, if not database schemas), it's fast, and it tends to work. Therefore, when something breaks, and human changes occurred around the same time, undo those changes as fast as possible, without waiting to prove that they're at fault.

My experience is that most people will want to argue that their change was safe, that it will make them miss their deadline, etc., etc.—or, if not argue, waste time debating the nuances of the root cause. You should try to ignore that noise. An outage isn't the time for nuance, and the deadline is virtually always less important than the breakage: just roll back! You can always roll forward again if it turns out to be something else.

Incident Response

When you're on call, once in a while, things are going to go really wrong, and you will have to organize an incident response—a coordinated team effort to mitigate a problem. For three years, one of my main jobs was leading the response to severe outages as an "incident commander." I worked on many tens of outages, some catastrophic, some minor—how many exactly I'm not sure. In this section, I'll discuss the best techniques for responding to outages that I've learned in that time.

In my experience, 99 out of 100 on-call pages are either non-problems or modest issues amenable to analysis and mitigation by a single engineer. Occasionally, things go wrong on a scale that can only be addressed by a team. At that time, we employ incident response techniques—standard processes for organizing a complex response to a problem, including assessing impact, running multiple parallel debugging efforts or mitigations, and communicating among ourselves and with stakeholders (like executives).

Incident response procedures exist in many types of organizations, from engineering to public relations to natural disaster management. Major problems are chaotic and frightening, and groups of people naturally respond chaotically, that is, inefficiently—in the worst outage I ever worked on, which lasted a devastating 1 hour and 40 minutes, we had forty panicked people on a video conference. Literally zero of them did the one thing we had thought of that might have actually helped.

Incident response is aimed squarely at that problem; it aims to ensure that a group of people partitions work, communicates, responds to changing circumstances, and learns after the fact, rather than all running toward the ball like toddlers at a soccer game.

That isn't to say that we seek to script every single thing a response team might do—some problems and responses are highly amenable to pre-planning, but the worst problems by definition require improvisation and autonomy; otherwise we would have automated them away already. We aim to explicitly define the methods that are highly likely to be needed in every problem, saving ourselves from deriving them on the fly—a command structure, communication system, and usually some critical domain-specific methods. The system should be tight and comprehensible—along the lines of the checklists detailed in Atul Gawande's fascinating *The Checklist Manifesto*.

Even for small teams, if you operate important software, you should have a plan for the event that something goes wrong. The next section has an example playbook you can use if starting from scratch.

Example Incident Response Playbook

Here are the areas I suggest for a basic incident response playbook:

- **Roles and how to assign them**: Avoid duplication and dropped balls.

- **Fast mitigation checklist**: Make it impossible to forget the most common and valuable interventions.

- **After-incident practices**: Use mistakes to make your technology and organization stronger.

Roles

The very first task in a major incident is to assign roles: responsibility for key parts of the response. Having explicit ownership for those roles, and a clear process for assigning them, can go a long way to prevent chaos; if this isn't codified, everyone will make an independent decision, and you'll have both duplication and gaps.

Here are the roles I've seen used highly successfully:

- **Incident commander**: Direct others. See the big picture, especially business priorities. This role should be assigned first, either to the first person on the scene or by a rotation. This person should focus entirely on identifying what needs to be done and directing others to do it—in my experience, doing any communication or debugging directly is a recipe for the overall breakdown of order.

- **Eyes [on dashboards]**: Monitor dashboards for changes in overall state of issue. Potentially extract certain specific metrics asked for by other team members.

- **Debugging/operations**: Flip switches, turn dials, and fix stuff. If needed, take the lead on digging into systems data to identify potential

Here's how I suggest assigning roles: the first person on the scene is always the incident commander. That person will assign all other roles as other engineers arrive on the scene, including possibly handing over the incident commander role if appropriate (e.g., if the first responder's skills are more urgently needed to do the direct mitigation or if you have a better IC on hand). If two people are on hand at the same time, someone should claim the IC role; if no one does, break the deadlock! You can say, "Rachel, let's make you incident commander starting now," and Rachel can step up and do her best.

Key Mitigation Checklist

At many companies and on many teams, a handful of key data and interventions will cover most (or many) problems. These should be on a simple checklist the team can examine in the heat of the moment. For example

- Check for recent deploys ➜ If you find any, roll them back.

- Check for high GC on the XYZ service ➜ Restart if found.

- Check for HW failure on master node ➜ Fail over to hot standby if needed.

- Check for datacenter-level networking failure ➜ Evacuate region if found.

After-Incident Practices

When a system I operate has an outage, the outage response isn't complete until what went wrong is understood in every detail—what failed, why it failed now, why mitigation did and didn't work, etc.—there should be no question about what happened during the incident that I'm not prepared to answer. Partly, that's because people are very likely to ask, and it's embarrassing to not be able to speak to failures in your own code. More to the point, however, it's because you'll dramatically deepen your understanding of the system and find real problems that you'll want to fix as system owner. I can say honestly that half of everything I know about distributed systems I've learned from going deep on outage analysis.

Many companies may ask teams to write an RCA (root cause analysis), AIR (after-incident report), or postmortem to formally capture failures and learnings; if so, you'll have a nice template ready to go. Failing that, you can roll your own—a simple 1–2-page writeup circulated to your team is often enough to capture key learnings.

You might ask—are people going to get mad at me? Will writing up what went wrong make me look worse, when things might just go away if I'm quiet? Well, maybe, in a dysfunctional organization. Healthy organizations don't punish honest mistakes, and they reward honesty and ownership. I've been fortunate enough to work at companies that have truly rewarded honesty and ownership with "blameless postmortem" culture; you should assume the best unless someone tells you differently. I'd start with total honesty to my manager and see what they think about the best way to communicate after a problem.

Fear, Excitement, and Learning

Outages are scary as heck; they've also taught me more poise and confidence than just about any other part of my job.

I've worked on more than just about anyone I know, and they still scare me from time to time—sometimes, you feel that only your own cunning can avert disaster, but you know you've already used every trick you know—it's pretty similar to the nausea of realizing you forgot your passport when you get to the airport.[2]

---

[2] I once found that I had already used all my tricks on 3 hours of sleep just as tens of thousands of customers were about to come online for a major event. I fully panicked. It worked out more or less fine.

The lucky thing is that if it gets that far, no one should blame you for only doing your best. If your backs are against the wall, your organization has already failed; after all, we aim to build systems that don't require dramatic interventions, and at a mature company, they should be required very infrequently. Therefore, when you find yourself improvising under pressure, you should see it as a theme park ride, an outage escape room—a little scary, a little tense, but also freeing. It's a chance to be completely in the moment, practice your grace under pressure, and improvise the best you can. I personally have found that the intense pressure has helped me achieve both technical insights, and a new confidence, that I might never have otherwise.

Incident Command in Detail

Incident command is the foundation of a response to a serious incident, and I'll discuss it in special detail—partly just because I happen to love leading outages and find it fascinating and partly because I've seen a number of engineers use this skill as a career springboard. My observations are drawn mostly from personal experience, but FEMA's Incident Command System training is an interesting reference as well. You can feel free to skip this section if you're unlikely to have to lead an outage.

Telling People What to Do

Software is a collaborative business, and we train ourselves carefully to build consensus and treat our colleagues respectfully and, indeed, gently; that means that for most of us, it's quite uncomfortable to give orders to colleagues we esteem. Nevertheless, do it! My experience is that when you're commanding an incident, people will sincerely appreciate it when you tell them what to do—because the team needs fast, crisp coordination. That doesn't whatsoever, by the way, mean that you shouldn't listen carefully (indeed, gratefully) to feedback from others; you're perfectly helpless without good observations and decisions from the team. However, when you're IC and think you know what needs to happen, it's your job to give clear, firm instructions.

Tracking the Threads

As Incident Commander, you're a brain; everyone else acts as your arms, legs, eyes, and ears. As an outage scales, you'll easily forget what threads you have going. A simple text file is the solution. Its only contents should be a list of the main debugging threads you have going so you don't lose track and can periodically keep others on track. For example, if a system is overloaded and you're trying to recover by a few methods at once (a contrived example, but bear with me):

- *Turning off app features*
- *Spawning new instances*
- *Divert some traffic to another region*

Establish a Rhythm

You should establish a steady rhythm of cycling between observation, analysis, action, communication, and review/summary; this predictable rhythm helps the team stay oriented and focused and particularly helps engineers joining the effort ramp up quickly. I do this with a simple checklist I call "The Incident Commander Loop."

Start:

1. Review status: Verbally review what's going on; get everyone on the same page.

"We've been seeing a 10% rate of HTTP 500s for loading the home page for the last 15 minutes; we believe this is due to partial DB corruption."

2. Look for mitigations: Do we know what might help? If so, do it. If not, get people digging in the areas that might help.

"Infra team, do you think we can attempt a rollback from snapshot? How long will it take us to assess that?"

3. Pull In others if needed: Do we have everyone we need? If not, go get them.

"If we can't, is it possible we could write a script to fix the data in-place? Dorian, can you please page someone from the inventory team?"

4. Pause a moment: Let everyone take a breath. If people are actively debugging, give them a few minutes to do it; set a timer on your phone. A small break contributes to a sense of order, which keeps people calm.

"Alright, we'll pause for five minutes while the inventory team works on the script. Everybody stay calm and take a breath."

Go to Start

Bus Factor > 1

You should never be the only person who knows something operationally important; if you are, you're putting your whole team at risk.

A production system is proof positive of the second law of thermodynamics; it constantly changes, seldom via central planning, trending irresistibly toward disorder as people make bug fixes, add features, change configuration, mitigate issues, and tune performance. As systems become more complex (and they seldom get simpler), knowledge becomes partitioned, and each individual engineer's view tends to become less complete and more stale. From a development perspective, that's an inconvenience, but operationally, it's a risk—the less complete your knowledge of a system, the greater your risk of breaking it as you change it.

Keeping everyone on a large team current on every aspect of an evolving system is impossible, despite the charming suggestion of The Mythical Man Month to keep a comprehensive dead-tree manual in every single office and update it every day. You should obviously do your part to make your team's documentation the best it can be. What I suggest on top of that is that every change that impacts the production environment or operations should be announced by email.

This unpopular position is designed to avoid disasters. When you're making a critical change, deploying, or responding to a problem, you usually don't reread the wiki first, even if it is up to date.[3] Therefore, when the operational environment changes—a new component is added, a tool's behavior changes, a zone becomes unavailable for failover, a component enters a shaky state—you need the information to be pushed onto operators' radar, not just available somewhere if they happen to look. An email gets that information where it needs to be, that is, top of mind.

Example: New Component

Subject: New User Cache Enabled

Hi Folks,

As of today, we've started rolling out a new cache of user data intended to improve page load performance. The design proposal can be found here. We'll be rolling out incrementally with this experiment config; in the event of a problem (such as seeing stale user data, which we believe to be very unlikely), you can feel free to set the rollout percentage to 0% with this configuration flag and reach out to Carlos and me. You can also see the rollout progress on this dashboard. Please feel free to reach out with any questions. Thanks!

Cheers,

Alice

---

[3]Which it should be, by golly.

Example: Operations Change
Subject: Load Shedding Config Change

Hi all,

As of today, our previous <u>load shedding configuration flag</u> has been supplanted by a <u>new config</u>; if you need to tune emergency load shedding, please use update the new flag. The interface is unchanged, but the flag controls some cases that were not previously covered. Our <u>operator wiki</u> has been updated as well. Please feel free to reach out with any questions.

Thanks,

Bob

Tests Should Always Work

A broken test suite is the beginning of the end of civilization. Broken tests mean guessing at what really works and doesn't; uncertainty about tests necessitates human testing; human testing means toil and outages; toil and outages mean a screeching halt to development velocity, and good engineers want to feel the wind in their hair. I'm therefore a zealot. I think every single test in a test suite should work all the time and that if a test breaks, it should be treated as a P1 bug without exception; breakages should be reverted just like any production breakage would be. If you compromise once, you can compromise twice, and if you compromise twice, you've created a culture of letting tests stay broken; hold the line.

I

Index

A

Adaptability, 46

Agile software development, 86

B

Bug report, 110

Burnout, 47, 48

Bus factor, 237–238

Business value, 116–117

C

Calendar, 73

Changing jobs
  how to, 42–43
  when to, 40–42

Circuit-breaking, 220

Code review, 203
  key considerations, 205–206
  receiving, 204–205
  reviewing, 204–205

Commenting, 198

Communication
  choosing a medium, 157–160
  core principles, 155–157
  receiving, 154–155
  technical writing (See Technical writing)
  theory of, 153

Compensation, 21–24
  bands, 21

Complaining, 146–147

Conflict

Conflict
  with a manager, 104–106
  resolution, 139–142

Context
  as core communication
      principle, 155–157
  technical writing, 164–166

D

Debugging
  common techniques, 209–211
  menu, 209–211
  philosophy of, 207–209

Dependency injection, 201–202

Disaster recovery, 217

Duplication vs. reuse, 200

E

Editing, 163–167

Email, 169–184
  archetypes
    operational risk, 177
    project status update, 177–179
    technical announcement, 175–176
  as a choice of medium, 158
  etiquette, 174
  links, importance of, 174
  mailing lists, 173
  "Remove Me From This List," 175
  replying on topic, 173
  signatures, 171–172
  strategy, 182

D. Heller, *Building a Career in Software*, https://doi.org/10.1007/978-1-4842-6147-7

Printed in the United States
By Bookmasters